UNDER THE BLOOD-RED SUN

by

Graham Salisbury

Teacher Guide

Written by

Jean Jamieson

Note

The Dell Yearling paperback edition of the book was used to prepare this guide. The page references may differ in the hardcover or other paperback editions.

Please note: Please assess the appropriateness of this book for the age level and maturity of your students prior to reading and discussing it with your class.

ISBN 1-56137-904-2

Printed in the United States of America.

To order, contact your local school supply store, or—

Novel Units, Inc.
P.O. Box 433
Bulverde, TX 78163-0433

Web site: www.educyberstor.com

Table of Contents

Skills and Strategies

Thinking

Comparing, evaluating, analyzing details, differentiating between fact and opinion, discerning the motivation of a story character

Comprehension

Predicting, comparing, story mapping, defining, sequencing, describing, point of view, character motivation

Literary Elements

Character analysis, setting, plot, figurative language, suspense, similes, synonyms, antonyms, opinions, personification, foreshadowing

Vocabulary

Target words, target word maps, use and effectiveness of words, synonyms, word comparisons, sorting, root/base words

Listening/Speaking

Participation in discussions, role-play, participation in dramatic activities, defending opinions, describing

Writing

Research, short paragraphs, captions, descriptions, short stories, add-on chapter, summarizing, propaganda

Summary of *Under the Blood-Red Sun*

December 7, 1941, is described as "a date that will live in infamy." (F.D. Roosevelt) Japanese war planes attack Pearl Harbor, Hawaii, and the distrust of all of those with Japanese ancestry begins. Tomi and Kimi Nakaji were born in Hawaii and are American citizens. Their parents and grandfather were born in Japan and come under scrutiny by those in governmental and military authority. After his father and grandfather are arrested, it is up to Tomi to uphold the family traditions and to honor the family name. With the continuing help and support of his friends, members of the Rats baseball team, Tomi assures his father and grandfather that he can *"watch out for Mama and Kimi. I can do it. I will do it."* (page 240)

About the Author

Graham Salisbury was born April 11, 1944, in Philadelphia, Pennsylvania. He grew up living on Oahu and on Hawaii, which are a part of the Hawaiian Islands, in a family in which the father was absent. Salisbury admits that he has holes in his life due to this, and he feels that this is one reason he writes about family relationships. Salisbury believes that authors should write about their feelings.

Salisbury received a B.A. from California State University at Northridge in 1974, and an M.F.A. from Vermont College of Norwich University in 1990. Salisbury recalls that he really did not choose to read until his first son was born. However, once he started, Salisbury became a voracious reader. This led to the urge to write stories of his own. Salisbury finds it easy to write about his own experiences while twisting realities and bending truths. For more information about Graham Salisbury, see page 247 of *Under the Blood-Red Sun.*

Background Information

Japanese Relocation

The attack on Pearl Harbor caused the United States to immediately enter World War II, and it also caused U.S. public and political opinion to turn against the Japanese. All Japanese were looked upon as capable of sabotage, and the success of the attack was assumed to be the result of espionage by Japanese Americans living in Hawaii and on the west coast of the United States. All residents of Japanese descent in Hawaii were rounded up and interrogated. On the west coast of the United States, a sort of hysteria began, creating a profound suspicion of Japanese Americans that quickly led to cries for their expulsion. On February 19, 1942, President Franklin D. Roosevelt signed Executive Order 9066, which called for the eviction and internment of all Japanese Americans.

The evacuation and incarceration of Japanese Americans began in April of 1942. Entire populations of Japanese-born, first and second-generation families were ordered to take only what they could hand-carry during the relocation. With less than a one-week notice, they were forced to leave behind their homes, jobs, savings, and income totaling about a half-billion dollars, along with land and farm equipment estimated at $70 million.

More than 40,000 Japanese, along with their 70,000 American-born children, were moved to one of ten hastily constructed relocation camps situated in desolate regions of the western and central United States. Conditions at the camps were austere and primitive.

Despite the harsh treatment accorded to the Japanese in America, 17,000 internees volunteered for military service. In total, more than 25,000 Japanese Americans proved their loyalty in uniform. On December 17, 1944, President Roosevelt announced the revocation of Executive Order 9066, thus assuring the return of the evacuees to the west coast. On December 18, 1944, the WRA made public its policy to terminate all centers under its control and to empty them within six months.

In the years following the internment of the Japanese Americans, efforts have been made to compensate them. The Japanese American Evacuation Claims Act of 1948 and its modification in 1951 resulted in less than 10% paid on the property losses of 26,568 claims. Attempting to remedy this situation, the government passed a bill in 1988 that did two things. First, the government apologized to Japanese Americans for the internment, also admitting that the relocation was not justified for security reasons. Second, the bill provided that each of the 60,000 internees or their descendants be paid a lump sum of $20,000.

Rationing

Government controlled rationing in the United States began in December of 1941, after the Japanese attack on Pearl Harbor. The emergency Office of Price Administration was created, with subsidiary boards staffed by volunteers. By the war's end the rationed items included automobile tires, automobiles, typewriters, bicycles, stoves, leather and rubber footwear, coffee, sugar, canned and processed foods, meats, fats, gasoline, fuel oil for home heating and coal. At the end of the war in 1945, rationing was generally eliminated.

Note: It is not intended that everything presented in this guide be done. Please be selective and use discretion when choosing the activities you will do with the unit. The choices that are made should be appropriate for your use and your group of students. A wide range of activities has been provided so that individuals as well as groups may benefit.

Introductory Information and Activities

Previewing the Book

Look at the cover of the book. What elements of the story has the cover artist, Kazu Sano, included in the illustration? What clues are given? Look at the faces of the boys. How do you think they are feeling? Are they worried, normal, thoughtful, pensive, etc.? Do you notice things in the picture that could elicit certain feelings? Discuss. What is the title of the book? What do you think that the relationship could be between the two boys? What do you think might happen next?

Guest Speakers and Volunteers

Senior citizen centers, high schools, junior colleges, universities, local governmental agencies, etc., have vital resources to share with their communities. Line up your guests before introducing the unit. For example: veterans of the Second World War, history scholars, local Senator or Representative, etc.

Material Collection

Collect books, periodicals, posters, pictures, etc. about the Second World War, Pearl Harbor, the relocation of Japanese-Americans, haiku poetry, Japan, and anything else that you wish to emphasize during the use of this novel and guide.

Personal Observations

Have students keep a personal journal for the recording of feelings and comments as *Under the Blood-Red Sun* is being discussed. This journal does not have to be shared. In addition, students may want to write about the devastation of war, the importance of friendship, peer support, etc.

Recommended Book List

Put up a large sheet of paper in the room. Ask that students fill in the requested information to share books that they would recommend to others.

Book Title	Author	Brief Summary

Bulletin Board

Forming groups of students with similar interests, use a bulletin board to go with an area of study. For example:

A. War
  - a) Cover the bulletin board with plain background paper.
  - b) Copy the following quotes to place on the board.
    1. "We are the citizens of the world; and the tragedy of our times is that we do not know this." (Woodrow Wilson)
    2. "All wars are civil wars, because all men are brothers...Each one owes infinitely more to the human race than to the particular country in which he was born." (Francois Fenelon, 1651-1715)
  - c) With the help of the students, eventually surround the quotes with the names of as many wars/conflicts that are brought to mind. (Names of some wars/conflicts: Hundred Years War, Battle of Towton, Massacre in Piedmont, First Dutch War, Second Dutch War, War of the Spanish Succession, Battle of Blenheim, French Revolutionary Wars, Battle of Jena, The Peninsular War, The War of 1812, The Napoleonic Wars, The Crimean War, American War of Independence [Revolutionary War], American Civil War, Franco–Prussian War, First World War, Second World War, Korean Conflict, Vietnam, etc.)

B. Pearl Harbor
  - a) Cover the bulletin board with background paper.
  - b) Place a map of the Hawaiian Islands on the board.
  - c) Place the date of the Japanese attack on Pearl Harbor on the board.

C. World War II
   a) Cover the bulletin board with background paper.
   b) Place a map of the world on the board.
   c) Highlight the European and Asian countries involved in the conflict.

Pre-reading Activity

Make a concept chart. At the center of a large sheet of paper put the word TRADITION. Use this paper to record student responses as they tell what this word means to them.

Pre-reading Discussion

Ask students to share family/cultural traditions they experience.

Using Predictions in the Novel Unit Approach

We all make predictions as we read—little guesses about what will happen next, how a conflict will be resolved, which details will be important to the plot, which details will help fill in our sense of a character. Students should be encouraged to predict, to make sensible guesses as they read the novel.

As students work on their predictions, these discussion questions can be used to guide them: What are some of the ways to predict? What is the process of a sophisticated reader's thinking and predicting? What clues does an author give to help us make predictions? Why are some predictions more likely to be accurate than others?

Create a chart for recording predictions. This could be either an individual or class activity. As each subsequent chapter is discussed, students can review and correct their previous predictions about plot and characters as necessary.

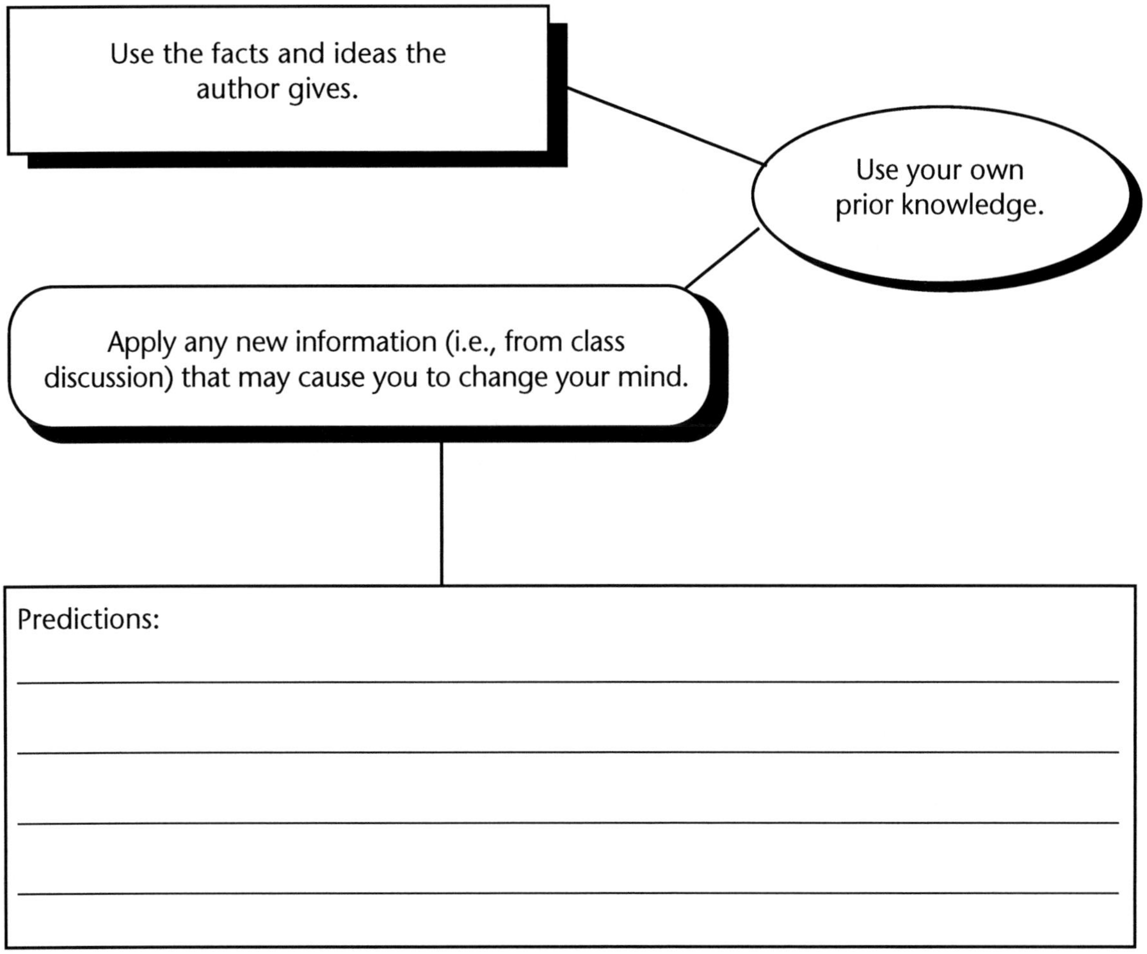

Use the facts and ideas the author gives.

Use your own prior knowledge.

Apply any new information (i.e., from class discussion) that may cause you to change your mind.

Predictions:

____

____

____

____

Prediction Chart

What characters have we met so far?	What is the conflict in the story?	What are your predictions?	Why did you make those predictions?

Story Map

Setting
Problem
Goal
Episodes
Resolution
Characters
Time and Place
Problem
Goal
Beginning → Development → Outcome
Resolution

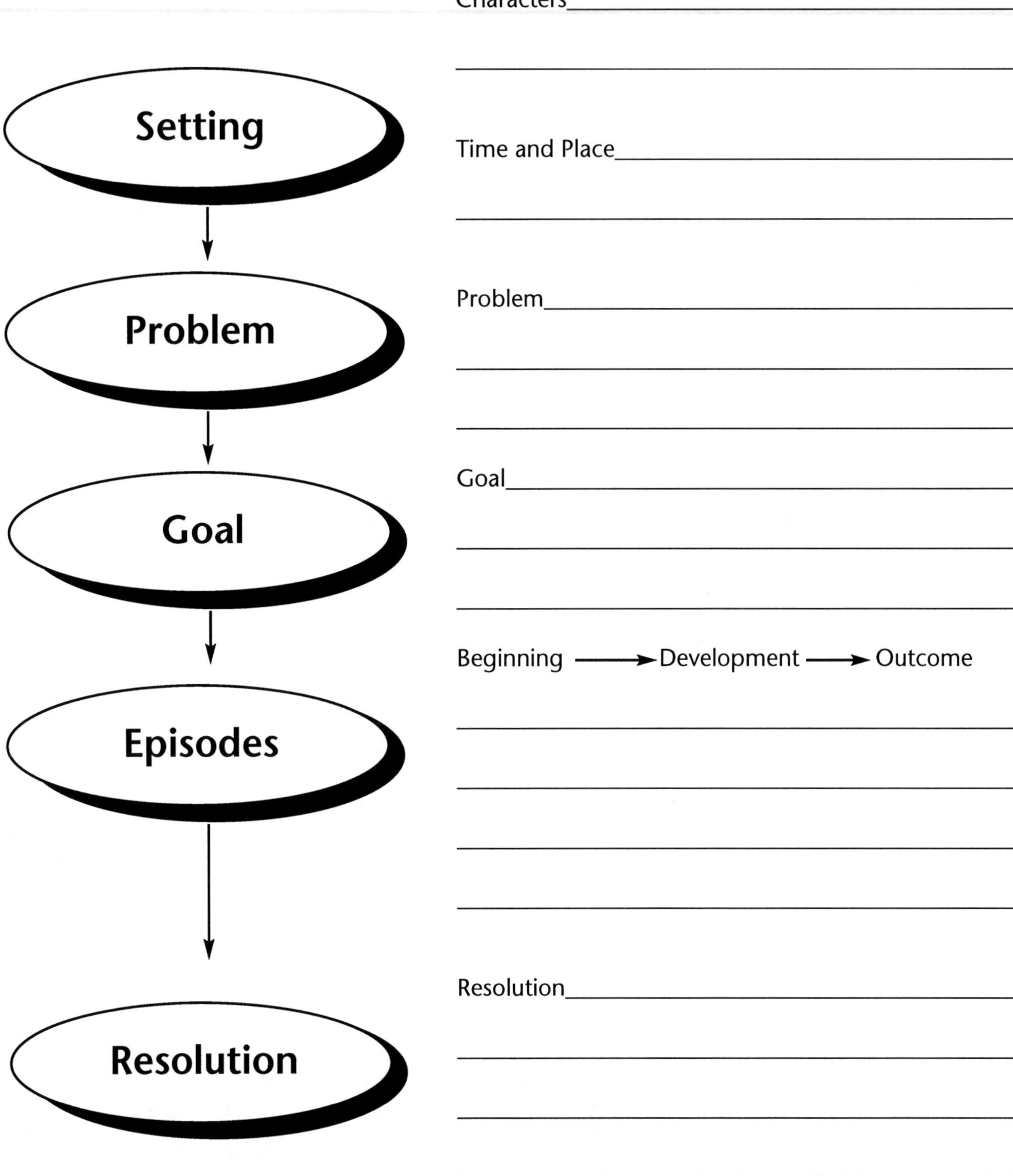

Using Character Webs in the Novel Unit Approach

Attribute webs are simply a visual representation of a character from the novel. They provide a systematic way for students to organize and recap the information they have about a particular character. Attribute webs may be used after reading the novel to recapitulate information about a particular character, or completed gradually as information unfolds. They may be completed individually or as a group project.

One type of character attribute web uses these divisions:

- How a character acts and feels. (How does the character act? How do you think the character feels? How would you feel if this happened to you?)
- How a character looks. (Close your eyes and picture the character. Describe him/her to me.)
- Where a character lives. (Where and when does the character live?)
- How others feel about the character. (How does another specific character feel about our character?)

In group discussion about the characters described in student attribute webs, the teacher can ask for backup proof from the novel. Inferential thinking can be included in the discussion.

Attribute webs need not be confined to characters. They may also be used to organize information about a concept, object, or place.

Attribute Web

The attribute web below will help you gather clues the author provides about a character in the novel. Fill in the blanks with words and phrases which tell how the character acts and looks, as well as what the character says and what others say about him or her.

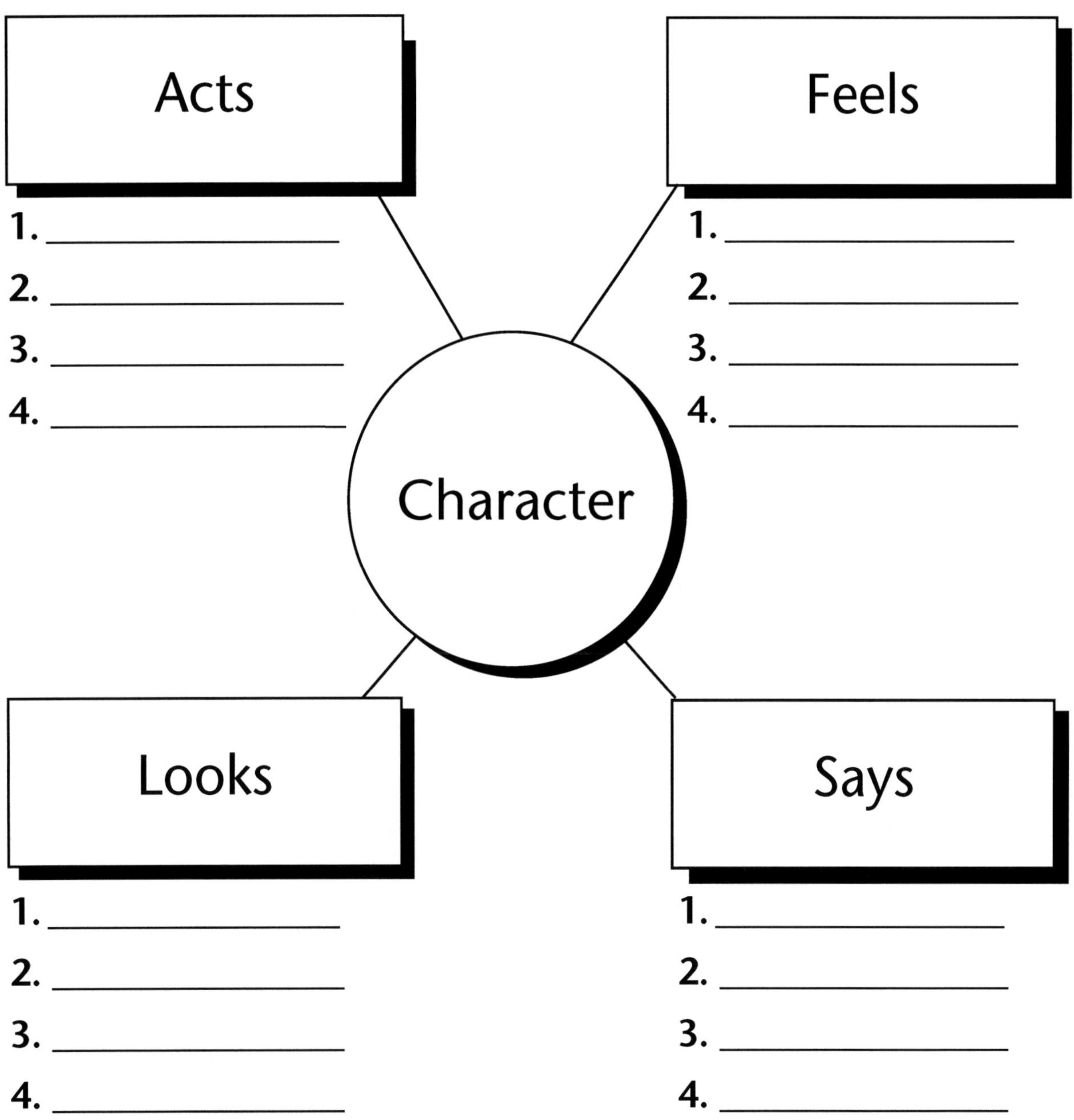

Attribute Web

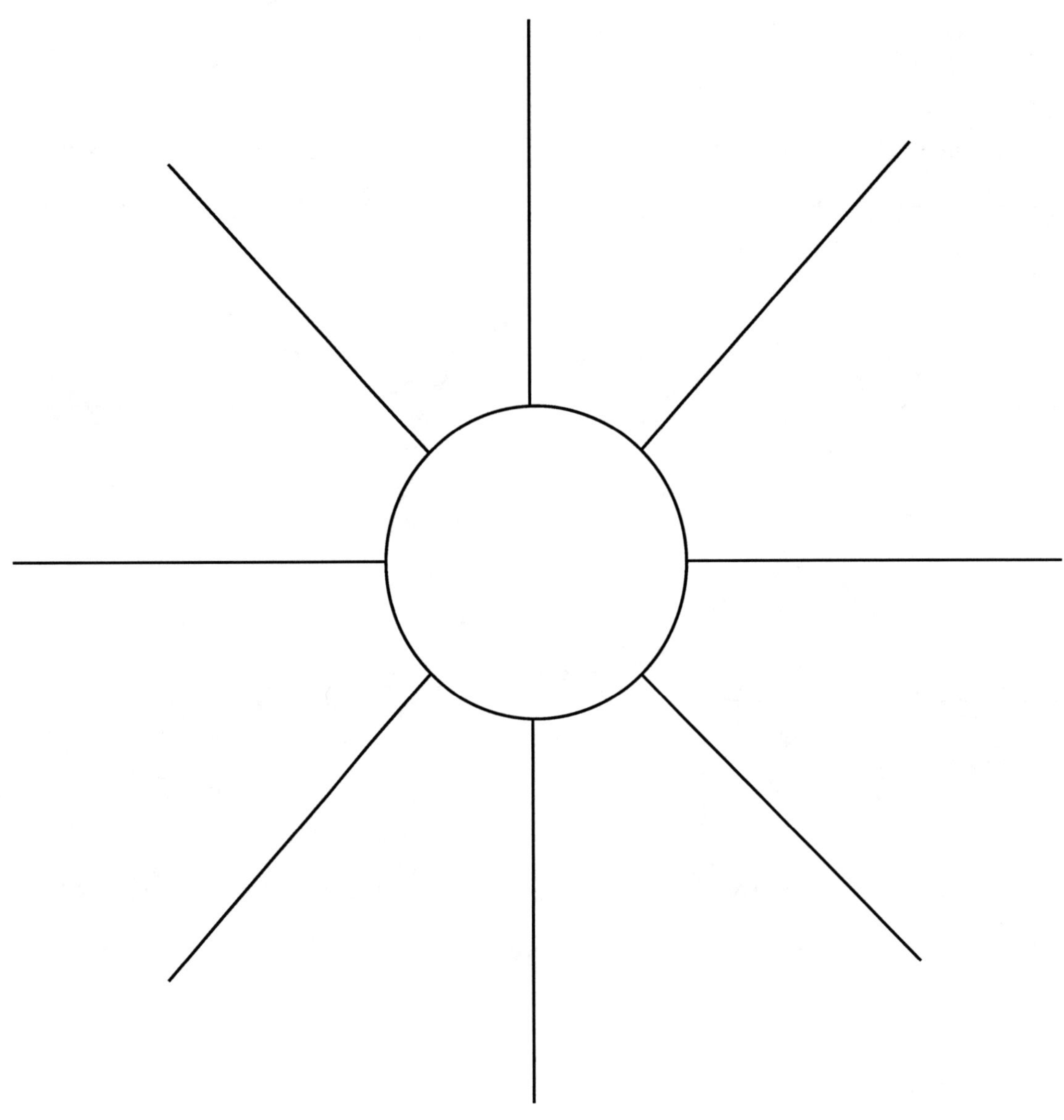

Vocabulary Activities

What is the Target Word?

Have the students act out some of the vocabulary words. Find out if classmates can guess the target words. Some suggested words for *Under the Blood-Red Sun* might include: clenched 3, squinted 4, descendants 6, inflexible 6, corrugated 6, lofts 6, humiliation 10, and slouched 11—selected from Chapters 1 and 2.

Target Word Map

Complete the following word map for target words. Some suggestions for *Under the Blood-Red Sun* might include: loomed 42, idled 46, wake 49, pursuit 51, swarm 53 and focus 61—selected from Chapters 5 and 6.

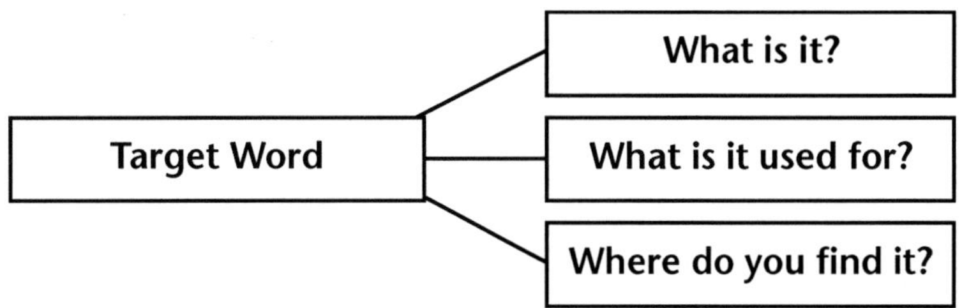

Alphabetize and Define

a) Select vocabulary words.
b) Alphabetize selected words.
c) Define each word according to use in the novel.

Use in a Sentence

a) Select a group of vocabulary words.
b) Use as many of the words as possible in one sentence.

Word Comparison

a) Choose two vocabulary words and explain how they go together.

_______________ and _______________ go together because

____.

b) Choose two vocabulary words and explain why they do not go together.

_______________ and _______________ are not usually related because

____.

Synonym Match

a) Select vocabulary words from a chapter under study.
b) List one synonym for each vocabulary word on a small piece of paper.
c) Mix the pieces of paper.
d) Match each synonym to the appropriate vocabulary word.

Root/Base Words

Find the base or root word for at least eight vocabulary words. Look at each word. What is the meaning of the root word? What is the meaning of the vocabulary word? What prefix or suffix has been added to the vocabulary word? How has the meaning of the root word changed by the addition?

Vocabulary Sort

Classify a group of vocabulary words into: names of things (nouns), action words (verbs), and describing words (adjectives and adverbs).

Odd One Out

Use vocabulary words from one or two chapters. Make a chain of four words. One word of the chain is the vocabulary word, two words are synonyms of the vocabulary word, and one word does not go with the others. (Mix sequence of words in chain.) Underline the word that does not belong with the others. Explain why it does not belong.

Word Use and Effectiveness

a) Select vocabulary words.
b) Group words by use.
c) Create a synonym train for each word.
d) Substitute a synonym for the vocabulary word in a sentence.
e) Compare the effectiveness of the thought conveyed.

Recommended Procedure

It is recommended that the book be read two chapters at a time. As each pair ends, predictions may be made as to what might happen next. These predictions are, in reality, good guesses based upon what has already happened in the story and on the clues given by the author. Predictions may be reviewed as the story continues. Knowledge of vocabulary words may be reviewed either individually or as a group by having students write or give simple definitions. These definitions may then be checked by seeing how the words are used in context as the story is read. If any definition is unclear, a dictionary may be used.

Chapter 1: "The Flag"—Pages 1-6
Chapter 2: "Crazy Boy"—Pages 7-16

Summary

It is early September 1941 on the Hawaiian island of Oahu. Grampa Joji decides to wash his large flag of Japan and to hang it on the clothesline to dry. By doing this, Grampa upsets the other members of the Nakaji family, who do not want to be thought of as anti-American. Thirteen-year-old Tomi Nakaji takes the flag down and shoves it up onto the porch. Tomi and his friend, Billy Davis, run to the field where Papa Nakaji keeps his racing pigeons. There they see Keet Wilson, who Tomi thinks of as "crazy boy," taunt and release the pigeons.

Vocabulary

tarp (1)	clenched (3)	squinted (4)	khaki (5)
immigrant (5)	descendants (6)	devotion (6)	inflexible (6)
corrugated (6)	lofts (6)	humiliation (10)	slouched (11)
grit (11) [feed]	irrigation (12)		

Discussion Questions

1. Who are the members of the Nakaji family? *(Pages 1-3, The members of the family are Grampa Joji, Papa, Mama, Tomi and Kimi.)* What does Grampa Joji do with his flag of Japan? *(Page 1, Grampa Joji washes the large flag and hangs it on the clothesline to dry.)* Why does this upset the other members of the Nakaji family? *(Pages 2-3, They do not want to be thought of as anti-American. Tomi reminds Grampa that the Second World War is being fought in Europe and that "Japan isn't making any friends around here.")* What do you think Tomi means by his statement about Japan?
2. How does Grampa Joji try to learn English? *(Page 4, He listens to the police on the radio.)* What is your opinion of this?
3. How does Tomi describe "the Japanese way" of Grampa? *(Pages 5-6, Tomi describes "the Japanese way" as being stern and obedient, working hard and being honest, and being inflexible.)* Which one of these attributes do you think is the most important? Why?
4. Who is "crazy boy"? *(page 6, Keet Wilson)* Why is he called "crazy boy"? *(Page 8, No one could stop Keet from going crazy. "When Keet got mad, he couldn't even stop himself. Not until somebody got hurt.")* Why do you think Keet terrorizes the pigeons and opens the loft door?
5. Although he wants to do it, why doesn't Tomi "pound Keet into the dirt"? *(Page 9, Tomi remembers the words of his father, "If you are troublemaker, then I am troublemaker...I am bad father, bad family. I no teach you to fight in the dirt like dogs!")* Do you agree or disagree with Mr. Nakaji's thinking? Why? Elaborate.
6. Has Tomi fought Keet in the past? *(Pages 12-13, Yes. The two were friends when Tomi was about nine. They fought over the possession of a knife.)* What was Papa Nakaji's reaction about the fight at that time? *(Page 13, Papa told Tomi, "You disgrace me. You fight and everyone think you troublemaker!")* What did Mama have Tomi do? *(Pages 14-15, Mama has Tomi think about his feelings whenever he hears Keet's name. She then asked Tomi if he would want others to feel that way when they hear his name.)* What do you think of Mama's way of explaining things to Tomi? Elaborate.

Supplementary Activities

1. Start character attribute webs for Grampa, Papa, Mama, Tomi and Kimi Nakaji, Billy Davis and Keet Wilson. Add to the webs as more is learned about them. *(Characterization is the way an author lets the reader know what the characters are like. In direct characterization, the author describes the character directly. In indirect characterization, the author provides clues about the character through thoughts, speech and actions.)*
2. Start a story map. (See page 9 of this guide.)
3. What was the status of the Hawaiian Islands in 1941? (Was it a monarchy, a democracy, a territory, or a state?) Do some research to find out. *(The Hawaiian Islands became a territory of the United States in 1900. Statehood was granted in 1959.)* Then broaden the research to include several historical events that are of interest to you.
4. As Grampa approaches Tomi, Tomi thinks that Grampa's "eyes said he wanted to wring my neck." (page 5) With a partner, take turns "speaking" to one another without using words.

Chapter 3: "Mose and Rico"—Pages 17-26
Chapter 4: "The Emperor"—Pages 27-40

Summary

Mose and Rico Corteles, cousins, and Tough Boy Gary Ferris, all of the Rats baseball team, are introduced, as is Mr. Ramos, their eighth grade teacher. The solidarity and bond of friendship between these characters is established. After school, Billy pitches to Tomi, and the boys talk about the wars that are raging in Europe, China and Japan. They are comforted by the presence of extensive military forces and equipment on their island of Oahu.

Vocabulary

fanatics (21)	reform (23) [school]	maneuvers (25)	convoys (25)
esteem (27)	mesh (30)	samurai (30)	symbol (30)
incense (32)	refuge (34)	sickle (34)	wary (37)

Discussion Questions

1. What is the name of the baseball team to which Billy and Tomi belong? Who thought up the name? Why did the boys form the team themselves? *(Page 18, The name of the baseball team is the Rats. Rico Corteles made up the name. The boys formed their own team because their school did not have a baseball team.)* Are you a member of a team? If so, why?
2. In addition to the sport, what is important about the Rats' team? *(Page 19, "But the thing about Mose and Rico, and Billy, too, was that they would stand by you no matter what. That was what the Rats were all about. Those guys were like brothers.")* Do you think this element is important to the sport, or is it limited to the personal lives of the players? Elaborate. Do you think all teams have this feeling of friendship and camaraderie? Explain.
3. How does Tomi describe Rico's way of going through life? *(Page 21, "An eye for an eye is the way Rico went through life.")* What do you think that means?
4. Why does Mr. Ramos prefer to be a teacher? *(Page 23, Once a lawyer, Mr. Ramos prefers to be a teacher so that he can help children before they get into trouble.)* What is your opinion of the decision Mr. Ramos has made?

5. Tomi, Billy, Mose and Rico talk about war. Billy asks, "Do any of you think we're going to get dragged into the war?" (page 24) How does Rico respond? *(Pages 25-26, Rico says, "Naah. Why us? The U.S. not bothering nobody." Rico goes on to elaborate, telling of many armed forces stationed on Oahu. When Billy relates Keet's feelings that the U.S. will be at war "before next summer," Rico says to remind Keet of the new aircraft carriers in Pearl Harbor.)* See Supplementary Activities, Facts and Opinions.
6. What do Mose and Rico give Billy? *(Pages 20-21, Mose and Rico give Billy a baseball.)* Why do you think Billy is pleased to receive a baseball from Mose and Rico? (page 27) Elaborate.
7. What does Tomi think about while riding on the bus? *(Page 28, Tomi thinks about what his father has told him with regard to trouble. Papa wants Tomi to "swallow trouble," to be above it, and to save face.)* What does Tomi think of his father, who follows his own advice? *(Page 28, "He must have been made out of steel.")* What do you think the phrase "swallow trouble" means? How could that be done?
8. What surprise, with regard to Lucky, does Billy have for Tomi? *(Page 31, Billy tells Tomi, "She's going to have puppies.")* Although happy about the puppies, why do you think Tomi feels he has to "act upset about it around Papa and Grampa"? (page 31)
9. Why does Mama think that there is "no one else in the whole world like Papa"? *(Pages 39-40, When Mama was sixteen she came to Oahu as a picture bride, to marry a sugarcane worker. Unfortunately, the worker was killed before Mama arrived. When Mama got off the boat, there was no one to take her in. She stayed with a fisherman and his bride. When Papa heard her story, he asked to meet the picture bride and married her.)* What will you add to Papa's attribute web?

Supplementary Activities

1. **Literary Analysis—Point of View:** Writers can tell their stories from many points of view. Sometimes a central character in the story tells the story. Sometimes the storyteller is a minor character. Sometimes the storyteller is a narrator who can see inside the characters, and sometimes the writer shifts the point of view from one person to another. Who tells most of the story of *Under the Blood-Red Sun*? *(Tomi)* Take one incident in the story and write about it from the point of view of a different character.
2. **Facts and Opinions:** Facts are statements that one can prove. Opinions are statements that tell what someone thinks about something. What is the opinion of Mose and Rico with regards to the financial status of *haoles*? *(pages 20 & 24)* What does Billy tell Mose and Rico? *(page 24)* What do the boys assume, based on an opinion, about the United States getting involved in the Second World War? *(page 26)* What might happen if one based a decision on an opinion? Elaborate.
3. Start character attribute webs for Mose, Rico and Mr. Ramos. (See pages 10-12 of this guide.) Add to all attribute webs as the story continues.
4. Tomi describes Tough Boy Gary Ferris as being "built like a garbage can." (page 27) Make a cartoon and illustration to go with this description.
5. Using the information given on pages 29 and 30 and previous information, make a Venn diagram to compare Tomi and Billy.

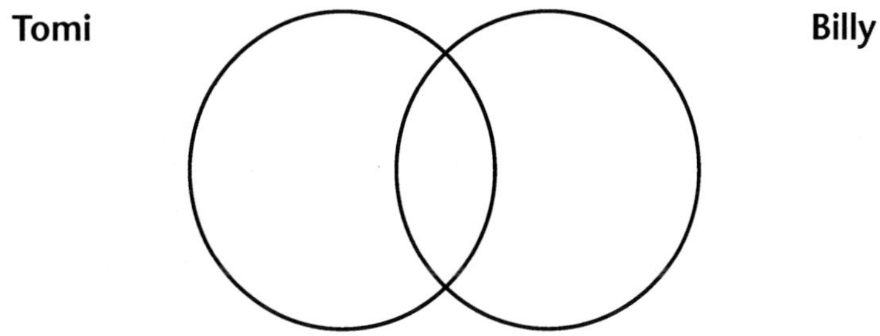

6. Tomi tries to imagine what it would be like to be one of the high-flying pigeons. "You could see so much it would make you dizzy." (page 39) What would the pigeons see flying over your area? Draw a bird's-eye view of your favorite section in the area. Label the buildings, etc.

Chapter 5: "The P-40 Tomahawks"—Pages 41-52
Chapter 6: "The Crowded Sea"—Pages 53-65

Summary

Papa and Sanji take Billy and Tomi on a fishing trip one weekend. The first day, Billy catches a very large yellow fin tuna on a line. It takes him five hours to bring the fish up to the boat. That night, Billy shares binoculars he has brought with Sanji, who is using them for the first time. The two investigate the moon and stars. Billy is the first *haole* that Sanji, nineteen, has talked with and the first *haole* to ride in his truck.

Vocabulary

loomed (42)	binoculars (43)	idled (46)	sampan (48)
tiller (48)	wake (49)	pursuit (51)	swarm (53)
frenzy (53)	mallet (55)	gaff (57)	focus (61)
averted (64)			

Discussion Questions

1. What does Billy's dad loan him for the fishing trip? *(Page 43, Billy's dad loans him a pair of binoculars.)* How do you think binoculars could be used on a fishing trip? Explain.
2. How does Papa act toward Billy? Is this behavior unusual for Papa? *(Page 44, Papa is friendly to Billy. Mr. Nakaji is friendly to everyone.)* Does Grampa approve of this behavior? *(Page 44, "It drove Grampa crazy, because he wanted Papa to be more firm, like he was. And anyway, Grampa wasn't too sure Papa should let me mix with haoles.")* Why do you think Grampa would not want Tomi to mix with haoles? Elaborate.
3. What are Billy and Tomi served for breakfast before the fishing trip? *(Page 44-45, Mrs. Nakaji serves the boys sticky rice and pours a mixture of raw egg and soy sauce over the rice.)* Why do you think Billy does not eat all of his breakfast?
4. What is Grampa's reaction when he sees Billy's uneaten breakfast? *(Page 46, "...Grampa clenched and flexed his jaw, and made his lips curl back to suck air in through his teeth. The tendons in his neck stood out like wires.")* From Tomi's description, how do you think Grampa is feeling?
5. What has Mama told Tomi and Kimi about the rice? *(Page 46, "Mama always told us never to leave even one grain of rice on the table, that it was a small treasure, that a farmer went through a lot of trouble to grow it.")* Do you agree or disagree with Mrs. Nakaji? Explain. Have you ever heard someone use a similar situation to encourage a child to eat everything on the plate? Record student replies of situations.
6. How does Tomi help Billy save face with Grampa? *(Page 46, Tomi tells Billy, "He's just telling you that if you want to be a muscle man like he is you gotta eat all your rice.")* What is something different Tomi might have said so that Billy would feel okay in the situation?
7. Who is Sanji? What is the meaning of the word sanji? *(Pages 46-49, Sanji is a nineteen-year-old fisherman who works with Papa on his boat. The word sanji means "three o'clock.")* What is Papa's opinion of Sanji? *(Page 48, "Papa thought Sanji was the greatest thing since diesel engines.")* To what might Papa compare Sanji at the present time?

8. Why doesn't Papa have a radio on his boat so that he can call for help if he needs it? *(Page 49, Papa cannot afford a radio for the boat.)* What might be some circumstances that could arise in which a radio would be a good thing to have on the boat? Elaborate. What would Papa have to do if he encountered trouble?
9. Why are the binoculars a special treat to Papa and Sanji? *(Page 51, They had never used binoculars before. Sanji thought the binoculars a "miracle.")* Do you recall how you felt the first time you looked through the lenses of binoculars? Elaborate.
10. What happens when two U.S. fighter planes see Papa's fishing boat? *(Pages 51-52, The pilots fly the fighters low over the boat, wag the wings of the planes, and then climb the planes high into the sky.)* Does the presence of fighter planes frighten the occupants of the boat? *(Pages 51-52, No. Papa waves to the pilots.)* Why do you think that is?
11. What does Sanji notice about the number of military planes in the area? *(Page 52, "You see lots of planes out here. Before, got one, two a week. But now, get maybe ten times that in one day.")*
12. What equipment do Tomi and Billy use to catch fish? *(Page 54, Tomi and Billy use a bucket that has line in it, with a hook and sinker on the end of the line. Bait is put on the hook, and the line is put overboard. The sinker takes the line down into the water.)* What do Sanji and Mr. Nakaji use to fish? *(Page 54, Mr. Nakaji and Sanji use poles.)* Which do you think you would prefer to use? Why?
13. How long does it take Billy to bring in his catch? *(Page 59, "It took about five hours.")* Why do you think it takes Billy that long? How do Papa and Sanji react to the time taken by Billy? *(Page 59, "And even though Papa and Sanji acted like they were irritated by missing out on more fishing, they let Billy finish the job. From the beginning they knew it would take that long.")* What is your opinion of the action of Papa and Sanji? Do you think it's important for Billy to "finish the job"? Why or why not?

Supplementary Activities

1. **Literary Analysis—Suspense:** Suspense is a state of mental uncertainty, excitement, or indecision. In literature, suspense is a quality of tension in a plot which sustains interest and makes readers ask "what happens next?" Suspense is what keeps readers interested in a story. Suspense occurs whenever we worry about the fate of a character. What is the element of suspense the reader is left with at the end of Chapter 6? What do you think the statement foretells?
2. **Literary Analysis—Foreshadowing:** Foreshadowing is used to provide a hint of what is to occur later. What do you think might be indicated by the inclusion of the incident of the fighter planes into the story? (pages 51-52)
3. Start an attribute web for Sanji. Add to it, and to the others, as the story continues.
4. How do binoculars work? Invite a volunteer to explain the workings of binoculars to the group. Compare objects viewed through the large and small lens of this optical device. Have groups create activities using binoculars as part of the equipment and then share these activities with others.
5. The plot is the action in a story. Usually a plot progresses through four stages—exposition, rising action, climax and resolution or the falling action. Make a diagram, similar to the one below, filling in the first steps. Continue to use the plot diagram for the remainder of the novel.

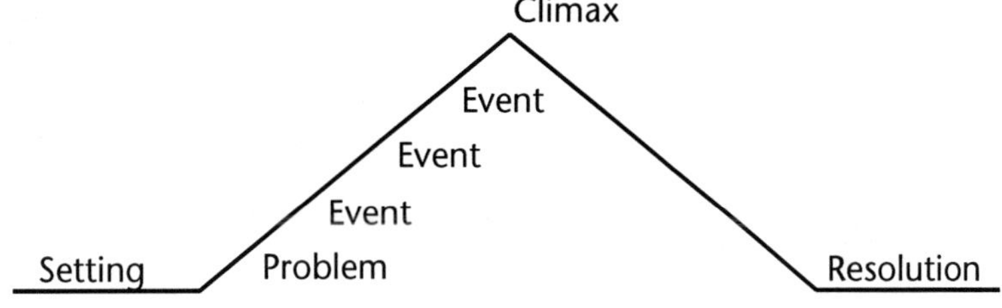

6. What kinds of military planes were being used by the United States in 1941? Do some research to find out. Choose one to study in depth. Share information with group members. Compare the military planes of the United States to those of other countries involved in World War II. Make conclusions.

Chapter 7: "Black Zenith"—Pages 67-76
Chapter 8: "Thunder on the Moon"—Pages 77-87

Summary

Billy and Tomi listen to Charlie's radio as the New York Yankees win the fourth game in the World Series of baseball. Grampa's waving of the Japanese flag irritates Mr. Wilson. News of the sinking of the USS Reuben James by a torpedo is published in the local newspaper. Lucky has four puppies. Billy chooses the smallest puppy to be his and names it "Red."

Vocabulary

machete (67)	dialogue (68)	rattled (74)	scornfully (79)
massive (85)	incredible (85)	eerie (86)	queasy (87)

Discussion Questions

1. What is Keet doing to get on Tomi's nerves? *(Page 67, Keet is "sneaking around," watching Tomi.)* What would Keet's behavior be termed at the present time? (See Supplementary Activities, Stalking.)
2. What does Charlie own that Grampa would like to have? *(Page 68, "...an old black Zenith radio that you could hear the police on...Charlie and Grampa listened almost every night.")* Why do you think Charlie and Grampa like to listen to the police on the radio? What do you like to listen to on the radio? Why?
3. Why does Grampa hate American baseball? *(Page 69, "He hated American baseball, because he couldn't understand what the radio said. Too fast.")* Do you think that by not understanding something people often come to hate it? Give examples.
4. Why does Tomi have to help his mother boil water in the backyard? *(Page 69, Tomi has to help boil water for washing clothes.)* Do you have responsibilities that directly impact your life and/or the lives of others? Explain.
5. What incident on the way to Charlie's house frightens Tomi? *(Page 70, A bullet is shot into a tree a few feet away from Tomi as he walks through the jungle to Charlie's house. Keet and Jake are playing in the jungle.)* Do you think Keet should have a rifle in his possession? What is your opinion of gun control?
6. Tomi and Billy listen to the broadcast of the fourth game of the World Series. What happens in the ninth inning of the game? *(Pages 73-74, The Dodgers think they have won, but on the last out the ball slips through the catcher's glove. The Yankees go on to win the game.)* How does Tomi feel about the game? *(Page 74, "And the Dodgers' spirit was broken—not to mention mine, because I knew Billy would never let me forget it.")* What additional events in the lives of Tomi and Billy might give them feelings of exhilaration or defeat?
7. What does Mr. Wilson say to Tomi when he calls Tomi over to his car? *(Page 78, "Listen to this, boy. You people are walking on mighty thin ice around here.")* What do you think Mr. Wilson means by saying "you people"? Do you think it is fair to attribute certain characteristics, features, etc. to others because a few have them? Why or why not?

8. What world event has happened to make Mr. Wilson angry? *(Pages 80-81, The Germans have sunk a U.S. destroyer, the USS Reuben James.)* Since Mr. Wilson can do nothing about the Germans, what does he do instead? Do you think this is something that he might do often? Elaborate.
9. Why does Tomi forget to tell his father about the puppies and the military maneuvers? *(Page 87, Papa tells Tomi, "Lot of people in Honolulu starting to point finger. They wondering whose side us Hawaii-Japanee going take, and what we going do if Japan and U.S. got into a fight.")* What do you think the general population is concluding? Why?

Supplementary Activities

1. **Literary Analysis—Personification:** Personification is the attributing of human characteristics to those things which are clearly not human. Graham Salisbury uses this technique often in the novel *Under the Blood-Red Sun*. For example: *"The car spit dust and little rocks out when it took off."* (page 79) Write an original short paragraph in which you use this technique at least twice.
2. **Stalking:** to pursue prey or quarry stealthily. Invite an officer of the law to explain a stalking offense to the group and the ramifications of such an act.
3. Lucky has four puppies. Mama tells Tomi, "If you can feed 'um, you can keep 'um." (page 83) Write out a different phrase that Mama might have used to convey the same meaning to Tomi. For example: "You must take care of the puppies so we can keep the wolf from the door." Make an illustration for the phrase.
4. There are some words and phrases in this section for which you may give your own interpretation based on the content of the story. Write definitions for the following and select additional words and phrases to add to the list: *thunked* (page 69), *tilly* (page 70), and *stink eye* (page 78).
5. Tomi mentions the names of some baseball players in the 1941 World Series. (pages 67-68) Choose one person who played baseball in 1941. It does not have to be a player on the Yankees or Dodgers teams. Imagine you are a sports reporter. Write a news report about that player.
6. Graph the favorite radio programs of the group members, or the categories of the programs, such as: music, news, sports, etc. Make summary statements from the graph.
7. Compare the housing amenities that you enjoy to those of Tomi in 1941. Such as:

Tomi	Me
kerosene lamps	electricity
outhouse	indoor plumbing

Chapter 9: "The Butcher"—Pages 89-97
Chapter 10: "Sunrise at Diamond Grass"—Pages 99-110

Summary

Mr. Ramos gets input regarding the science projects of the students in his eighth grade class. After school, Tomi, Billy, Mose and Rico take the city bus to go to see the new pitcher for the Kaka'ako Boys work out. Keet shoots out a window of his father's new car. Tomi hears Mr. Wilson yell at Keet as he delivers eggs to the Wilsons' house. Seeing and hearing an angry Mr. Wilson frightens Tomi. On Sunday, Billy and Tomi meet at diamond grass for baseball practice. As they get started, they hear the roar of engines and see dark fighter planes. The boys climb the banyan tree and witness the bombing of Pearl Harbor. (Pearl Harbor, an American naval base in Hawaii, was attacked by Japanese on Dec. 7, 1941. The next day the United States declared war on Japan.)

Vocabulary

pronunciation (90) cringed (100) vise (102) abruptly (107)

Discussion Questions

1. What science projects do Tomi, Billy, Mose and Rico choose to do for Mr. Ramos' class? *(Page 22, Tomi chooses to do a demonstration on pigeons. Page 89, Billy chooses to do a demonstration and explanation about throwing curve balls. Page 90, Mose and Rico will work together to make a volcano and show how it works.)* Which of these projects would interest you the most? Why? What is something different that you might choose to do for a science project? Elaborate.
2. When the four boys are walking to the city park, they are stopped by a gang of seven Japanese boys blocking the way. Which one of the four boys is not allowed to pass by the gang? Why? *(Page 93, Billy is not allowed to pass because he is a haole.)* Why do you think the gang members do not like haoles?
3. What is the nickname of the new pitcher for the Kaka'ako Boys? What is his one pitching flaw? *(Page 96, The new pitcher is called "the Butcher." When he pitches, he is not always on target.)* Why do you think the Rats do not want Billy to show the Butcher how to get better aim? *(page 96, opinion)*
4. What does Tomi overhear when he delivers eggs to the Wilsons' house? What is Tomi's reaction to it? *(Pages 100-102, Tomi overhears Mr. Wilson's anger directed at Keet. Tomi is frightened. "The ugliness in Mr. Wilson's voice was meaner by far than anything Keet had ever even tried to aim at me.")* Dramatize pages 99-102.
5. What name does Kimi choose for one of Lucky's puppies? *(Page 103, Kimi names one of the puppies Azuki Bean.)* What is an azuki bean? Why do you think Kimi chooses that name for the puppy?
6. Tomi and Kimi play with the puppies for a long time. What does Tomi forget to do? Who does he blame for his forgetfulness? *(Page 103, Tomi forgets to let the pigeons out, which he is supposed to do every afternoon. "All because of Keet Wilson. Or Grampa...yeah, Grampa.")* Do you think Grampa is to blame for Tomi's forgetfulness? Why or Why not? Explain.
7. Where are Billy and Tomi on Sunday morning? Why are they there? *(Page 104, On Sunday mornings, Billy and Tomi meet at diamond grass to practice pitching, catching and batting.)* What is something different that happens on this Sunday morning? What do they do? *(Pages 105-110, The boys see low-flying planes and hear gun fire. They climb the banyan tree to get a better look at what is going on. They see the bombing of Pearl Harbor by the Japanese. They run to Charlie's to listen to the radio.)* What do you think of the way Billy and Tomi react to the air raid by the Japanese planes? Do you think you would have done anything differently? If so, what? Elaborate.

Supplementary Activities

1. **Literary Analysis—Similes:** Similes are comparisons using the words like or as. Find three similes in this section. Copy them from the book, make note of the page numbers, and tell what is being compared in each instance. Make up a simile of your own and explain the comparison.

2. With reference to the volcano and the accompanying report, Rico tells Mose, "I make it, you fake it." (page 91) Make a captioned cartoon that illustrates:
   a) a different reply that Rico might have made to Mose,
   b) an alternative situation between Mose and Rico, or
   c) an alternative situation between two of the story characters of your choice.
3. Do some research and summarize the events of the attack on Pearl Harbor. For example: A surprise attack on Pearl Harbor by Japanese forces at 7:55 on the Sunday morning of December 7, 1941, forced the United States into World War II. Vice-Admiral Chuichi Nagumo led a 33-ship Japanese striking force that steamed, under the cover of darkness, to within 200 miles north of Oahu. His carriers launched about 360 airplanes against the Pacific Fleet, under Admiral Husband E. Kimmel, and the Hawaiian ground troops under Lt. General Walter C. Short. Chief targets were eight American battleships among the 92 naval vessels anchored in the harbor. Three of the eight battleships stationed there were sunk, one was run aground, and one was capsized. The other three were also damaged. Eleven smaller ships were destroyed or damaged badly, 169 aircraft that were on the ground were destroyed, 1,178 people were wounded and approximately 2,403 people died. The attack on Pearl Harbor was one of the most successful and daring military actions that had ever been executed. With one attack, the Japanese seemingly reduced the United States from a naval power to a weakling. With the U.S. out of the way, Japan thought the Pacific was theirs. "Remember Pearl Harbor" became the rallying cry for the United States in World War II. That same day, Japan also conducted strategic strikes on the Philippines, Guam, Midway, Hong Kong, and Malaya. U.S. President Franklin Delano Roosevelt called it "a date that will live in infamy." The United States declared war on Japan on the following day. Hitler did not believe the news when he first heard it and thought it was a propaganda ploy. When the news was verified, he and Mussolini declared war on the United States.
4. Create a U.S. newspaper headline for December 7, 1941.
5. What techniques does the author use to keep your attention as the bombing of Pearl Harbor occurs? Make a list of the words that are used to describe the sounds heard by Billy and Tomi. Add to the list at least five words that might be used to describe the sounds and at least five words that might be used to describe what is seen by the boys. Use some of these words in an original descriptive paragraph.

Chapter 11: "Jackhammers"—Pages 111-122
Chapter 12: "Messenger Birds"—Pages 123-131

Summary

Charlie, Billy and Tomi listen to the radio and hear, "This is no maneuver...This is the real McCoy!" The three hook up garden hoses at Billy's house, in case a fire should start after the bombing takes place, and Tomi returns home. Azuki Bean is the only thing that calms Kimi. Grampa places eggs on the doorstep of the house, expecting Japanese soldiers to arrive. It is American soldiers who come. Everyone is questioned about parachutists and about someone signaling Japanese planes during the bombing. Charlie comes over to tell the Nakajis about the blackout rule. Grampa goes to the cemetery where jackhammers are being used to break up the ground so the dead can be buried. The next morning, one army man and two policemen arrive at the Nakaji house. Grampa and Tomi are ordered to kill all of the pigeons. Mrs. Wilson does not allow Mama into the Wilson house to work. Mama and Tomi go to the store, but are only able to purchase a small bag of rice and six onions. Keet continues his observation of the Nakajis.

Vocabulary

jackhammers (111)	shrapnel (113)	martial law (119)	blackout (119)
slug (124)	saboteurs (130)	apprehended (130)	infractions (130)

Discussion Questions

1. What do Billy and Tomi hear announced on Charlie's radio? *(Page 112, "This is no maneuver...This is the real McCoy!")* What happens as they are listening to the radio? *(Page 112, The bombing starts up again.)* What do Tomi, Billy and Charlie do? *(Pages 112-113, They drag six garden hoses up to Billy's house, in case of fire.)* Where does Billy think they should be? *(Page 113, "We'd be better off hiding in the jungle. They're not going to bomb trees.")* Do you agree or disagree with Billy? Why?
2. When Tomi gets home, where does he find Kimi? *(Page 115, Tomi finds Kimi hiding in Mama's closet.)* What is the only thing that will bring Kimi out of the closet? *(Page 115, Tomi gets Azuki Bean for Kimi to hold.)* Why do you think this works? Do you think anything different would persuade Kimi to leave the closet? Elaborate.
3. Why does Grampa arrange fresh eggs in a line on the top step of the Nakaji house after the bombing stops? *(Page 117, Grampa is ready to give the eggs to Japanese soldiers he thinks will be coming to the house.)* Who arrives instead? What do they want? *(Pages 117-118, "Eight U.S. Army guys charged toward us with rifles and bayonets pointing at our stomachs." The men have received a report that someone in the area has been signaling the Japanese planes.)* Who do you think might have made the report? Why?
4. What news does Charlie bring to the Nakaji house? *(Page 119, The territory is under martial law and there is a blackout in effect.)* What is martial law? *(Page 119, General Short is the governor of the islands.)* What is a blackout? *(Page 119, No one can have any light showing through from the inside of a building.)* Why do you think these two measures are put into place? Explain.
5. After everyone is asleep that night, where does Grampa go? Why? *(Pages 121-122, Grampa hears jackhammers being used and goes to investigate. Army men at the cemetery are using jackhammers to dig graves for those killed at Pearl Harbor.)* What is Tomi's reaction when Grampa tells Tomi what he has seen? *(Page 122, "Bodies? It hadn't even occurred to me that people had been killed down there.")* Do you think that Tomi's reaction is common or uncommon? Why?
6. What happens at the Nakaji house early Monday morning? *(Page 123, An army man and two policemen arrive at the door of the house.)* Why have they come to the house? *(Page 124, The Nakajis are told, "Someone reported that you kept messenger pigeons...How long have you been sending messages to the enemy?")* Who do you think might have made such a report? Why?
7. What are Grampa and Tomi instructed to do with the pigeons by the army man? *(Page 125, They are told to destroy the pigeons.)* Do you agree or disagree with this decision by the army man? Why?
8. What happens when Mama goes to work at the Wilsons' house on Monday? *(Page 129, Mrs. Wilson will not let Mama in the house.)* Why do you think Mrs. Wilson does this? Do you think that Mrs. Wilson is justified in doing this? Why or why not?
9. Does Mrs. Wilson's reaction seem to be a common feeling by non-Japanese people? What happens when Tomi and Mama wait in line at the grocery store? *(Page 131, As Tomi and Mama wait in line to get into a grocery store, a lady stares at them. "What she saw was a Japanese boy, and his Japanese mother.")* What do you imagine these non-Japanese people are thinking?

Supplementary Activities

1. **Literary Analysis—Character's Motivation:** A character's actions often tell the reader something about the character's thoughts and feelings. What do you think might be Keet's motivation for spying on Tomi? (page 131)
2. The U.S. Army and police are searching Oahu for those who might be friendly with the enemy after the bombing of Pearl Harbor. (pages 117 & 123) Is there a difference between espionage and sabotage? Explain your answer.
3. Keep a continuing written record of incidents mentioned in the story that indicate anti-Japanese-American sentiment. Give your opinion of each incident.
4. Make a list of synonyms for the words *sabotage* and *spy.* (Example follows.) Choose six additional words that you would associate with war and list antonyms for those words as well.

    sabotage: subvert, disable, incapacitate, undermine, sap, wreck, vandalize, damage, hamper, obstruct, hinder, scotch...

    spy: scout, reconnoiter, watch, follow, shadow, trail, stalk, eavesdrop, oversee, snoop, pry, search, investigate...
5. Tomi tells of the first night of the blackout. "With the whole island blacked out, it was the blackest of black nights." (page 120) Imagine your room blacked out. Write a description of how you feel.

Chapter 13: "Rumors"—Pages 133-142
Chapter 14: "Red"—Pages 143-153

Summary

On Tuesday morning, Charlie explains the anti-Japanese, anti-Japanese-American position taken by the army and FBI to Mama, Grampa and Tomi. Charlie advises Grampa, Mama and Tomi to stay close to home. Mama and Grampa go through the house, collect everything of Japanese tradition, and bury it nearby. Tuesday night Grampa rides off on his bicycle, to return Wednesday morning with the news that Papa is in jail with a bullet wound to the leg, Sanji has been killed, and Papa's boat has been sunk in the canal. A few days later, Tomi gives Red to Billy and helps Jake and Billy construct a bomb shelter. Billy and Tomi get in some ball practice once again.

Vocabulary

disgraced (133)	revenge (135)	kimono (136)	curfew (136)
traditional (137)	considering (138)	sympathizers (138)	quivering (141)
camouflaged (149)	smirked (153)		

Discussion Questions

1. Unable to sleep on Monday night, Tomi checks on Grampa. What does Grampa say to Tomi in Japanese? *(Page 133, "We have been disgraced.")* What do you think Grampa means by this statement? To what does it refer? What is the meaning of the word disgrace? *(Disgrace: dishonor, discredit, defame, shame, humiliate, tarnish...)*

2. What news does Charlie bring to Tomi, Mama and Grampa on Tuesday morning? *(Page 135, Charlie informs Tomi, Mama and Grampa that the army and FBI are arresting Japanese men. "They say they help plan for attack Pearl Harbor...They say the fishermens been taking fuel out to submarines...They going to arrest all the fishermens." Page 136, "The paper said today, they going shoot any boat come toward the island if no got one U.S. flag on top.")* What do you think are some pros and cons of these decisions? Discuss with others. Have a debate.
3. What advice does Charlie have for Tomi, Mama and Grampa? Why? *(Page 135, Charlie advises Tomi, Mama and Grampa to stay close to home. "Everybody nervous about Japanee, and lots of people with guns and machete out there. They looking for revenge...They say: you never know about them." [the Japanese])* What name might be given to this spreading of ideas and information that is injurious to a group of people? *(propaganda)* How does propaganda work?
4. After Charlie leaves, what decision does Mama make? *(Page 137, Mama tells Grampa and Tomi, "We going through this house to find everything that could bring trouble...photograph, letter...everything...We going bury 'um.")* Do you agree or disagree with Mama's decision? Why or why not? What might be the consequences if this plan is not carried out?
5. What two things does Grampa hide in the jungle? *(Page 137, Grampa takes the altar and the family sword to hide in the jungle.)* Where does Tomi bury the rest of the things? *(Page 137, Tomi buries the rest of the things in a burlap bag under the house, near the Japanese flag.)* Which place do you think is the better hiding place, the jungle or under the house? Why?
6. Who does Tomi meet up with near his house after burying the things? *(Page 138, Tomi meets up with Keet and Jake.)* What happens? *(Page 139, Keet and Jake have a fight. Keet leaves and Jake tells Tomi that it was Keet who "told the police about your birds.")* Are you surprised to learn that it was Keet who told about the birds? Elaborate. What do you think will happen to the relationship between Jake and Keet?
7. Ignoring the curfew, Grampa goes to Kewalo to get news of Papa. He returns the next morning. What news does he bring home? *(Pages 141-142, Papa has been shot in the leg and taken to jail, and the boat has been sunk in the canal. Sanji has been killed. The Americans shot at the boat because it did not display an American flag.)* What is your opinion of this action? What might have been an alternative?
8. After learning of Papa's fate, Tomi tries to be practical. What are some of Tomi's concerns? *(Page 144, Tomi wonders what they are going to do, especially if the Wilsons will not allow the family to stay in the house. Tomi knows that the eggs from Grampa's chickens will not bring in enough money. He wonders if he could get a job after school, but what could an eighth-grader do?)* What practical suggestion would you make to Tomi?
9. What does Kimi see sitting on one of the lofts? *(Pages 144-145, Kimi sees two of the three lost pigeons.)* What is Tomi's concern about the pigeons? *(Page 145, Tomi is concerned about Grampa's reaction to the return of the pigeons.)* What does Grampa do when he comes outside? *(Page 146, Grampa stands at the top of the stairs, hands in pockets, raises his chin toward the sky and says to Tomi, "Good, nah?")* By doing this, do you think Grampa is saying something to Tomi about the pigeons? Explain.
10. Just before Christmas, Tomi takes Red over to Billy. What do the boys do to cement the crack in their relationship? *(Pages 152-153, They go to diamond grass to practice pitching and catching.)* How do you feel about the relationship between Billy and Tomi at this time?

Supplementary Activities

1. Kimi is concerned about the absence from home of her father. Tomi suggests to her that they talk with Papa. Kimi wants to know how they will be heard. Tomi tells Kimi, "I think he can hear every whisper that comes from here." (Tomi taps Kimi's heart.) "All you have to do is close your eyes and think about what you want to say." (pages 143-144) Help Kimi. Write a poem to Papa for her. Use the quatrain poetry form. A quatrain is a poem written in four lines. It may be rhymed or unrhymed. When rhymed, the pattern of the poem is left up to the discretion of the writer.
2. Soon after the bombing of Pearl Harbor, the newspapers reported that "local Japanese who wanted to sign up couldn't, that they weren't loyal to the U.S." (page 149) Do some research. Report on subsequent Japanese-American involvement in the Second World War. (The Japanese-American soldiers were about 17,000 in number. The tasks that they performed in the war included intelligence operations and combat. When they fought, they were segregated into regiments of Japanese-Americans only and did not fight in the Pacific. The most decorated American combat unit, the 442nd Regiment [popularly known as Go for Broke] was made up of Japanese-Americans.)
3. Billy tells Tomi why they have not been together for so long. Billy says to Tomi, "You want to know why I didn't come see you for so long?" (pages 150-151) What is Billy's concern? How does he resolve this problem? What is your opinion of Billy's way of resolving the problem? Is there something different you would suggest to him?

Chapter 15: "Shikata Ga Nai"—Pages 155-164
Chapter 16: "Mari"—Pages 165-170

Summary

Mose, Rico and Tomi walk to the police station. They find out that Papa Nakaji is probably being held on Sand Island, but is not allowed visitors. Returning home, Tomi searches for Grampa and finds him in the jungle with Charlie. Grampa has the family sword out and is grieved that Japan has brought shame to the family. Billy is given his father's binoculars for Christmas and brings them along when he, Tomi and Mama visit Sanji's wife and young daughter. The little girl, Mari, is fascinated by the binoculars. Billy gives them to Mari before he leaves.

Vocabulary

averted (156)	hesitantly (156)	rationed (157)	wardens (157)
trench (159)	pyramids (159)	pushy (160)	canteen (165)
barges (166)	tact (167)	indebted (170)	relieved (170)

Discussion Questions

1. What friends come to see Tomi after the bombing of Pearl Harbor? *(Page 155, Mose and Rico come to see Tomi.)* Do you think anything in their friendly relationship has changed? Elaborate.
2. As the boys walk together, they talk about people being scared and confused after the bombing of Pearl Harbor. (pages 157-159) What do you think would cause these feelings?

3. Where do the three boys go, and why do they go there? *(Page 157, The boys walk to the police station. They want to find out where Papa Nakaji is being held.)* Are the boys able to get any information? *(Page 161, Yes. They are told that Papa Nakaji is probably on Sand Island. They are also told that no one can see him.)* Why do you think the police officer relented and gave Tomi some information? *(opinion)*
4. Later that day, where does Tomi find Grampa? Why is Grampa there? *(Pages 162-163, Tomi finds Grampa in a bamboo forest near their house. Charlie is with Grampa. Grampa is there to get the sword he hid on December 7.)* What feeling does Grampa have about the sword at this time? *(Page 163, Grampa feels that Japan has disgraced the family sword.)* Why do you think Grampa feels this way? *(opinion)* Do you agree or disagree with him? Why?
5. Billy comes to see Tomi after Christmas. What does he bring along? *(Page 165, Billy brings the binoculars. His father has given the binoculars to Billy for Christmas.)* What does Tomi tell Billy when asked if he had Christmas? *(Page 165, Tomi tells Billy, "Yeah, we had it.")* Tomi knows that he has told Billy a lie and doesn't know why he did it. Why do you think Tomi lied to Billy? *(opinion)*
6. When Mama tells Tomi they are going to go downtown to see Sanji's wife and daughter, what does Billy ask of Tomi? *(Page 167, Billy whispers to Tomi, "You think I could come with you?")* What does Tomi do in reply? *(Page 167, Tomi asks, "Mama...can Billy come too?")* After that, why do you think Billy tells Tomi, "Somebody's got to teach you a little tact"? (page 167) What is tact?
7. What is the name of Sanji's daughter? *(Page 169, Sanji's daughter is named Mari.)* How does Billy get Mari to look through the binoculars? *(Page 169, Billy gets down so that his eyes are level with Mari's. He looks through the binoculars and then asks her if she would like to have a look. With Billy's help, Mari uses the binoculars.)* What do you think of Billy's treatment of Mari? Since he has no younger brothers or sisters, how do you think Billy knows about younger children?
8. Before he leaves, what does Billy give to Mari? *(Page 170, Billy gives the binoculars to Mari.)* Why does Billy take the bananas that Reiko offers to him? *(Page 170, Billy takes the bananas because Tomi has encouraged him to do so, so that Reiko will "feel better.")* What is it that Reiko will really "feel better" about? *(Page 170, Reiko will not feel indebted to Billy for the binoculars.)*
9. On the way home, why do you think Mrs. Nakaji tells Billy, "You nice boy, Billy...You welcome our house anytime"? (page 170)

Supplementary Activities

1. A proverb is a short, popular saying that expresses some obvious truth. Tomi tells Rico and Mose, "You should see the looks we get from the people now. They think we're spies or something." (page 157) Read the following African proverb. What does it mean to you?

   There is no discrimination in the forest of the dead.
2. As Tomi prepares to look for Grampa, Tomi whistles for Lucky. "That dog—she always made me feel good." (page 162) Why do you think that is?
   a) Interview pet owners.
   b) Do some research about people and pets.
   c) Share your information.
3. The location of Sanji's wife's place is described at the bottom of page 167. The inside of the apartment is described on page 168. Read the descriptions and make an illustration of one of them. How do you think the people living there feel about it? Write a fictional short story about someone else who lives in a place like the one in the descriptions.
4. On page 157, the rationing of gasoline is mentioned. Find out more about the rationing of some items by the U.S. after the bombing of Pearl Harbor.

Chapter 17: "Sand Island"—Pages 171-181
Chapter 18: "Tough Guys"—Pages 183-194

Summary

Tomi walks to the harbor. He swims to Sand Island, unseen in the rain. Tomi creeps up to the compound and manages to get the attention of a fisherman-friend of Mr. Nakaji. Papa comes near to Tomi's hiding place and advises Tomi to go back home after it is dark. Papa sends a message to Mama that she should not worry. Tomi falls asleep and swims back after dark. The long swim back tires Tomi. He falls asleep on the ledge of the bridge and is awakened by a soldier. Tomi explains himself satisfactorily and is driven home by two soldiers.

Vocabulary

muffled (172)	barricades (172)	convoy (172)	entry (173)
restricted (173)	whirlpools (174)	reef (175)	dutiful (176)
respectful (176)	obey (176)	blotch (179)	sprinted (180)
lunged (180)			

Discussion Questions

1. What is Grampa's reply when Tomi says he wants to go to Sand Island to see if Papa is there? *(Page 171, Grampa says, "You go there, they going shoot you.")* Do you agree or disagree with Grampa? Why?
2. Why does Tomi duck under an arched concrete bridge at the harbor? *(Page 173, The rain "lets loose" as he starts to return home after being sent away by guards.)* What does Tomi realize as he looks at Sand Island? *(Page 174, Tomi realizes that there is no barbed wire under the bridge and none on Sand Island.)* What does Tomi decide to do? *(Pages 174-175, Tomi decides to swim to Sand Island.)* What is your opinion of Tomi's decision? Elaborate.
3. Before he goes into the water, what does Tomi do with his ID card? Why? *(Page 174-175, Tomi sticks his ID card into a crack on the ledge of the bridge and then covers it with his sweatshirt. He thinks, "If I lost that I'd be in more trouble than I wanted to think about.")* What kind of trouble might that be?
4. Does Tomi reach Sand Island? *(page 175, yes)* What continues to go through Tomi's mind as he goes to the flat land above the beach? *(Page 176, Grampa's words go through Tomi's mind: "They going shoot anybody try go there...")* What does Tomi think in response? *(Page 176, "Grampa was right. I should just be dutiful. I should be respectful and obey everything he says.")* Do you agree or disagree with Tomi? Why?
5. What does Tomi do? *(Pages 176-177, Tomi continues his search. He sees the camp and runs across an open field to three trees surrounded by tall weeds. Hiding in the weeds, Tomi sees no movement in the camp. He waits.)* Does Tomi's patience reward him? What happens? *(Pages 177-178, Men come out of one building and disperse. One man, who knows Papa, comes near Tomi. Tomi calls to the man, who goes to get Mr. Nakaji.)* Do you think that if someone came by who did not know Mr. Nakaji, things would go differently for Tomi? Elaborate.
6. What does Papa tell Tomi? *(Pages 178-179, Papa tells Tomi to be quiet, to stay in the trees until nighttime and then go back, to tell Mama not to worry, and that he, Tomi, is very brave.)* Although Tomi wants to talk with his father, what does he do? *(Page 179, Tomi remains quiet.)* How difficult might it be for Tomi to be quiet?

7. What happens to Tomi near the bridge as he returns to Oahu? *(Pages 180-181, The sucking motion of the motor of a passing tugboat threatens Tomi's life.)* How does Tomi escape? *(Page 181, Tomi dives down toward the bottom of the river to get away from the motion of the tugboat.)* What is the consequence of this occurrence? *(Page 181, Tomi is exhausted. After he gets on the ledge of the bridge, he unknowingly falls asleep.)* What are some events that could take place as Tomi sleeps? See Supplementary Activities #1, Cliffhanger.
8. Tomi is awakened by a member of the Military Police. After Tomi is identified, what does the MP tell him? *(Page 184, "Count yourself lucky this time.")* How do you imagine Tomi feels when he hears these words?
9. How does Tomi get home? *(Pages 184-185, Tomi is driven home in a jeep by two soldiers.)* Why? *(Page 184, The MP who found Tomi tells him, "I don't want anyone shooting a kid.")* If the MP had not felt this way, what are some things that might have happened to Tomi?
10. How does Grampa react to Tomi's news, "I—I saw Papa"? *(Pages 186-187, Grampa calls Tomi a liar, and says, "You no can do!")* What could explain Grampa's disbelief?
11. Are Mama and Grampa angry with Tomi? *(Pages 187-188, No. They were afraid for Tomi. Mama tells Tomi, "We need you, Tomi. We all need to be together, to help each other.")* Although Tomi arrived home safely, what are some alternative consequences of his actions? See Supplementary Activities, #4, What If.
12. Do the Rats and the Kaka'ako Boys gather for the baseball game on New Year's Day? *(page 193, yes)* How does Tomi feel about the game as he and his friends walk to the park? *(Page 191, Tomi feels it is wrong to be playing baseball with his father imprisoned only a mile away. However, he feels good about being with his friends.)* Is Tomi the only one in this or a similar situation? What do you think children like Tomi, who have a parent or parents imprisoned, should do?

Supplementary Activities

1. **Literary Analysis—Cliffhanger:** A cliffhanger is a device used, often at the end of a chapter, to increase suspense. The reader is "left hanging"—eager to read on and to find out how a situation will be resolved or to find out what a mysterious statement means. What is the cliffhanger at the end of Chapter 17 on page 181? Make a list of different ways in which this situation might be resolved. Discuss your resolutions with other class members. As the story continues, find out if anyone came up with the same resolution used by the author.
2. On page 172, Tomi describes the scene at the harbor: "All around the water—everywhere—were barbed wire barricades wound in twisted and jumbled coils from post to post, the wire going all over like it was spun by a lunatic spider." Make an illustration of your interpretation of this description.
3. As Tomi swims on his back near the harbor at night, he sees "stars by the millions." Seeing these peaceful stars makes Tomi feel sad and lonely. (page 180) Using the poetry form of your choice, write an original poem that expresses a sad, lonely feeling.
4. A change in one circumstance may alter the outcome of a story. Consider the following situations:
    - What if Tomi had not gone to Sand Island?
    - What if Tomi had been arrested on Sand Island?
    - What if Tomi had been injured by the tugboat?

   Add to the What If situations. Choose one to use as the basis for a short story.

5. Foreshadowing is indicating or suggesting events beforehand. Foreshadowing provides a hint of what is to occur later. Write a short paragraph that tells what might be foreshadowed by the last paragraph of Chapter 18 on page 194. Was there a previous incident that foreshadowed this one? Explain. (pages 92-94)

Chapter 19: "The Kaka'ako Boys"—Pages 195-204
Chapter 20: "Lucky"—Pages 205-214

Summary

The Rats win the baseball game. The gang members surround the Rats after the game, and the fighting starts. However, the gang backs off when the Kaka'ako Boys make their presence known. Tomi and Billy persuade Grampa to join them for batting practice. With Kimi as a spectator, Grampa is thrilled when he hits a ball about five feet on his second try. Lucky and her puppies dig up Grampa's flag. After a frantic chase, the boys retrieve the flag and bury it under a pile of stones. Mrs. Wilson asks Mama to come back to work. Grampa rides his bike downtown. The Sand Island prisoners have been sent to the mainland.

Vocabulary

strutting (196) lurked (205)

Discussion Questions

1. What happens after Tough Boy gets hit by a ball pitched by the Butcher? *(Page 197, Tough Boy accepts the apology of the Butcher and the offer to let Tough Boy punch the Butcher should it happen again.)* What is Tomi's reaction to this situation? *(Page 197, Tomi wants to shake the hand of Tough Boy.)* Why do you think Tomi wants to do this? *(Opinion—answers will vary.)*
2. Why do the members of the Rats team think they have been cheated out of a run? *(Page 198, The ball Rico hits lands in the outfield and rolls right up to where the Coral Street punks are sitting. One of the gang members tosses the ball to the infield. Rico has to stop on third rather than go on to home plate.)* What do the Kaka'ako Boys offer to do? *(Page 199, They offer to play the inning over.)* What might be a reason that the Rats don't want to do this?
3. What are two personal things the Rats find out about the Butcher during the game? *(Page 197, The Butcher has an unnaturally high voice. Page 202, The Butcher's name is Gayle.)* Does anyone tease the Butcher about his voice and name? Why? *(Page 202, The Butcher is not teased; probably because of his size.)* Do you think the Butcher would be teased about his name and voice if he was smaller in size? Why or why not?
4. Which team wins the ball game? *(Page 203, The Rats win the ball game.)* Who surrounds the Rats as they prepare to leave? What happens? *(Page 203, The gang members surround the Rats. A fight ensues.)* Why does the fight stop as quickly as it started? *(Page 203, The Kaka'ako Boys arrive and the gang members back off and slowly walk away.)* What words and phrases might be used to describe the Coral Street gang?
5. With reference to the Kaka'ako Boys (page 204), why does Tomi think, "Criminy, I was going to miss those guys"? *(Pages 189-190 & 193, Some of the Kaka'ako Boys have had to get jobs, so this is their last game. Tomi realizes that he will have to get a job too.)* Do you think any of the baseball players will keep in touch with one another? If so, who would be most likely to do so? Who would be most likely to be left out? Why? *(Opinion—answers will vary.)*

6. Mama is worried that Grampa will have another stroke. She tells Tomi that he will have to help Grampa with the work, so that Grampa has time to relax. What does Tomi want Grampa to do? *(Page 208, Tomi wants Grampa to come along while he and Billy practice.)* What does Grampa want Tomi to do for him? *(page 208, clean the chicken coops and sell the eggs)* Does the work Grampa wants done seem reasonable?
7. Why does Tomi think Grampa can be irritating at times? *(Page 208, Grampa keeps Tomi waiting while making up his mind.)* What are some things people do that might be irritating to others?
8. What makes Kimi and Grampa laugh while they are at diamond grass? *(Pages 208-209, Tomi asks Grampa to bat the ball.)* Why do you think Grampa eventually tries? *(Opinion—answers will vary.)*
9. Does Grampa hit the ball? *(Page 210, Yes, on the second try, Grampa hits the ball about five feet.)* What is Grampa's reaction? *(Page 210, "Grampa started jumping up and down like a crazy man." Grampa laughs and gets everyone laughing at his antics.)* What does the laughter do for everyone?
10. What do the dogs dig up? *(Page 210, The dogs dig up the buried flag of Japan.)* After they retrieve the flag from Lucky and Red, what do Billy and Tomi do with it? *(Page 211, The boys bury the flag under a pile of stones.)* Do you think that is a safe place for the flag? Why or why not? See Supplementary Activities #2.
11. Where does Grampa ride on his bicycle the next morning? Why? *(Page 212, Grampa rides downtown. He has heard that the men from Sand Island are to be sent to the mainland. Grampa wants to try to ask somebody about it.)* What does Grampa find out? *(Page 214, Grampa tells Mama, "They gone already...Mainland.")* What does Mama tell Tomi they will do? *(Page 214, "We going be strong, that's what...We going wait and we going be strong.")* What will you add to Mama's attribute web?

Supplementary Activities

1. Make a list of as many things as you can think of that might happen to Grampa's flag buried under a pile of stones. Choose one. Write a short story that includes the flag in that situation.
2. Do some research about the benefits of laughter.

Chapter 21: "The Katana"—Pages 215-226
Chapter 22: "Not Far From Pearl Harbor"—Pages 227-244
Epilogue: Pages 245-246

Summary

As Grampa is taken away by two men from the FBI, he tells Tomi to take good care of the family sword and the family name. Charlie shows Tomi where Grampa has hidden the sword and leaves. Looking for a different hiding place for the sword, Tomi is threatened by Keet. Tomi boldly faces Keet and takes the sword as he leaves. Papa sends a postcard to the family, with a message to each member. School opens and Mr. Ramos helps the students understand that power is freedom to make choices.

Vocabulary

evacuated (215)	futon (220)	censor (227)	jumble (238)
relocated (245)	survivors (245)	espionage (245)	

Discussion Questions

1. What happens to Grampa two days after Papa is sent to the mainland? *(Pages 216-217, Grampa is taken away by two men.)* What does Grampa tell Tomi as he is being dragged to the car of the two men? *(Page 216, Grampa tells Tomi to save the katana [family sword], and to protect the family name and not to disgrace it. [translated on page 218])* Why do you think Grampa tells Tomi this and not something else? *(Opinion—answers will vary.)*
2. What does Tomi do immediately after Grampa is taken away? *(Page 217, Tomi immediately blames Keet and Mr. Wilson for Grampa's seizure. He bangs on the door of the Wilson house, but no one is home.)* How does Billy help Tomi? *(Page 217, Billy grabs Tomi and pulls him into the trees. While doing this, Billy talks to Tomi quietly and tries to calm him down.)* What do you think might have happened if Billy had not been with Tomi?
3. With what previous situation does Mama compare the present one? What does she tell Tomi about them? *(Page 219, Mama tells Tomi, "When I first came to this islands was more worse than this...I could survive then, and we can survive now.")* What tasks does Mama assign herself, Kimi and Tomi? *(Page 220, Mama will work for Mrs. Wilson, Kimi will do Grampa's chickens, get the eggs and sell them, and Tomi must find work to make a little money to help.)* Does this seem reasonable? Why or why not?
4. Why does Tomi go to see Charlie the next day? *(Page 221, Tomi hopes that Charlie knows where Grampa hid the katana.)* Is Charlie able to help Tomi? *(Page 222, Yes, Charlie takes Tomi to the hiding place in the jungle.)* What responsibility does Tomi feel as he holds the sword? *(Pages 222-223, Tomi feels that Grampa counts on him to save the family sword for those of the past, the present and the future.)* Do you think Tomi will be up to this responsibility? Why or why not?
5. Tomi takes the sword and goes deeper into the jungle. What happens when Tomi stops to look at the sword again? *(Pages 223-225, Keet Wilson, aiming his .22 rifle at Tomi's head, has Tomi put the sword on the grass. Keet fires at the sword, nicking the handle. Although Keet threatens to shoot Tomi, Tomi picks up the sword and places it in the scarf and bag, and then Tomi backs into the jungle with the sword.)* How would you describe the behavior of each boy?
6. How does Tomi respond to Keet's taunt of telling his dad [Mr. Wilson] about the sword? *(Pages 225-226, Tomi tells Keet that he is not stupid enough to tell anyone about the sword. If he did, Keet would have to deal with Tomi, who tells Keet that he would be made to "pay for it...and not in money.")* What do you think Tomi means by this? Is Tomi's threat to Keet successful? Why do you think Tomi gets the results that he does?
7. When does the family hear from Papa? *(Page 227, The family receives a postcard from Papa near the end of January.)* What message does he have for each family member? *(Page 228, Mama is not to worry. Kimi is to help Mama. Grampa is to watch the boat. Tomi is to find a job, to feed the pigeons, and to help Sanji's family.)* What doesn't Papa know about?
8. School opens, and Mr. Ramos asks the students, "Does anyone have any idea why this happened? Why the Japanese attacked Pearl Harbor?" What are some of the answers the students give? *(Page 233, "They wanted to sink our ships." "Because they don't like us?")* What answer would you have given to Mr. Ramos?

9. What reason does Mr. Ramos give for the attack by the Japanese? *(Pages 233-234, "But the real reason—the reason at the bottom of all the wars in the history of human life—is power.")* How is **power** defined in their class? *(Page 235, Power is "freedom to make our own choices.")* Explain how "freedom to make our own choices" is power.
10. What do Rico, Mose, Billy and Tomi do after school? *(Page 237-238, They go down to the canal and locate Papa's boat.)* From looking at the boat, what observations do the boys make? *(Page 238, There are bullet holes in the deck. The deck is submerged. Everything looks rusty and old. The boat is full of water, so it would be heavy to drag up. Even if they got the boat up, no one could use it because of the war.)* Relate the sinking of the boat and not being able to use it to the concept of power.
11. What does Tomi do when he is insulted by a man working on a car? *(Page 241, Tomi explains to the man, "You got it wrong, mister. I was born here. I live here, just like you do. And I'm an American.")* How does Tomi feel after he speaks to the man? *(Page 241, Tomi feels strange, almost peaceful inside.)* What has Tomi done?
12. What good news does Billy share with his friends? *(Page 242, Billy can stay at Roosevelt the following year.)* Why has the school plan changed? *(Page 242, Plans have changed because Mr. Davis now wants what Billy wants.)* What do you think has brought about the change in Mr. Davis?
13. Why does Tomi decide to clean up the *katana* that night? *(Page 244, Tomi wants to share the katana with Kimi and tell her its story.)* Why do you think Tomi feels it is the right time to do this? *(Opinion—answers will vary.)*

Supplementary Activities

1. Form groups. Choose and dramatize significant chapters/sections of the book.
2. Complete the attribute webs.
3. Complete the story map.
4. Choose one story character. Write a summary that is a continuation of that character's life. Elaborate on one incident.
5. Read and discuss the Epilogue on pages 245-246.

Conclusion

Discuss the following saying with the group:

Man's inhumanity to man makes countless thousands mourn.

Post-reading Questions

1. What is friendship? List student responses.
2. What qualities do you think make a person a good friend? Make an attribute web for the word FRIEND.
3. Do you think Tomi and Billy will remain friends throughout the duration of the Second World War? ...Longer?
4. Read the following adages about friends and friendship. Add to the list with the sayings suggested and created by the students. (An *adage* is a saying about a common observation. Each adage has been passed on through the years, and the author of the adage is unknown.)
    - Friendship is to be purchased only by friendship.

- The light of friendship is like the light of phosphorus, seen when all around is dark.
- The only way to have a friend is to be one.
- Friendship is the only cement that will ever hold the world together.
- A friend is one who knows all about you and still likes you.
- A friend is one who comes to you when all others leave.

5. What are some of the things over which Tomi and his family have no control and which change and/or influence their lives?
6. Theme (the novel's central idea)
   a) What is the author's message?
   b) Why do you think the author wrote this story?
   c) What do you think is the most important thing to remember about this story? Why?
7. Personal Opinion
   a) Which story character can you identify with the most? Why?
   b) What is your opinion of the ending of the novel?
   c) Do you feel that all of the issues raised by the author were resolved? Explain.
   d) Would you want to change something about this story? Elaborate.
   e) Would you recommend this novel to others? Why or why not?
8. Look at the illustration on the cover of the book. Has the cover artist depicted Tomi and Billy as you have pictured them from the description in the story? Is there something you would change? Why or why not?

Post-reading Extension Activities

1. Read and discuss the book *Faithful Elephants* by Yukio Tsuchiya.
2. Possible Areas of Study from Bulletin Board Projects:
   A. War
      a) causes
      b) weapons
      c) personnel
      d) ramifications
   B. Pearl Harbor
      a) Timeline: Pearl Harbor

   [Timeline courtesy of Tri-City Chapter 31, Pearl Harbor Survivors Association]

   0342: Minesweeper CONDOR sights periscope off Honolulu Harbor and notifies patrol destroyer WARD to investigate.

   0458: Minesweepers CROSSBILL and CONDOR enter Pearl Harbor. A defective submarine net remains open.

   0600: 200 miles south of Oahu, carrier ENTERPRISE launches 18 aircraft to scout ahead. Aircraft are to land at Ford Island, Pearl Harbor. Their ETA is 0800.

   0610: 220 miles north of Oahu, Admiral Nagumo orders the launching of the 1st wave of 183 aircraft off six carriers. 2 are lost during takeoff.

0630: Destroyer WARD is again notified of a submarine sighting, this time by supply ship ANTARES off the Pearl Harbor entrance. A Navy patrol plane is dispatched to the scene.

0645: WARD opens fire on target, hitting conning tower, as she closes in and drops depth charges. Air attack by Navy patrol plane follows.

0653: WARD'S commander, Captain Outerbridge, sends message to the Commandant of the 14th Naval District: "We have attacked, fired upon and dropped depth charges upon a submarine operating in defensive sea area."

0700: Commander Fuchida, flying towards Oahu, directs his pilots to home in on local radio station.

0702: Privates Lockhard and Elliott of Opana Radar Station pick up what appears to be a flight of unidentified aircraft bearing in 132 miles north of Oahu. Discussion follows.

0710: Elliott phones in information to Fort Shafter. The only person present at the Information Center is Lt. Tyler, having begun his on-the-job-training on Dec. 3. The conversation lasts ten minutes.

0715: Capt. Outerbridge's attack message, delayed in decoding, is delivered to the duty officer of the 14th Naval District, and to Admiral Kimmel's duty officer. The Japanese launch a 2nd wave of 168 assault aircraft.

0720: Lt. Tyler feels certain that the unidentified planes are B-17s, scheduled to arrive from the mainland. He instructs the Opana station to shut down. Privates Elliott and Lockhard, however, continue to plot the incoming flight.

0733: Important message from General Marshall from Washington to Short is received via RCA in Honolulu. Unfortunately, the cablegram has no indication of priority. The messenger, Tadao Fuchikami, proceeds with the normal routine.

0735: A reconnaissance plane from cruiser CHIKUMA reports that the main fleet is in Pearl Harbor.

0739: Opana Station loses aircraft on radar 20 miles off coast of Oahu due to "dead zone" caused by surrounding hills.

0740: The 1st wave of Japanese aircraft sights the North Shore of Oahu. The deployment for attack begins.

0749: Commander Fuchida orders attack. All pilots are to begin assault on military bases on Oahu.

0753: Fuchida radios code to entire Japanese Navy, "TORA TORA TORA," indicating success of the maximum strategic surprise. Pearl Harbor is caught unaware.

0755: Island-wide attack begins. Japanese dive bombers strike the airfields at Kaneohe, Ford Island, Hickman, Bellows, Wheeler and Ewa. Aerial torpedo planes begin their run on ships in Pearl Harbor.

0800: B-17's from the mainland reach Oahu after 14-hour flight. Aircraft from carrier ENTERPRISE arrive at Ford Island. Carrier and planes are caught between enemy and friendly fire.

0802: Machine guns on battleship NEVADA open fire on torpedo planes approaching her port beam. Two planes are hit. However, one missile tears a huge hole in ship's port bow.

0805: Repair ship VESTAL, moored outboard of battleship ARIZONA, opens fire. Admiral Kimmel arrives at CINCPAC headquarters. Battleship CALIFORNIA receives second torpedo "portside at frame."

0806: Prompt action is directed by Ensign Edgar M. Fain and prevents the ship from capsizing. High level bombers begin their run "on both bows" of ships in battleship row.

0808: KGMB radio interrupts music calling for: "All Army, Navy, and Marine personnel to report to duty." High level bombers unleash armor piercing, delayed action bombs from altitude of 10,000 feet, scoring hits on battleships.

0810: Forward magazines on battleship ARIZONA suddenly ignite, resulting in a tremendous explosion and huge fireball sinking the battleship within nine minutes. The concussion of the explosion blows men off of repair ship VESTAL.

0812: General Short advises entire Pacific Fleet and Washington, "Hostilities with Japan commenced with air raid on Pearl Harbor."

0815: KGMB interrupts music with 2nd call ordering all military personnel to report for duty.

0817: USS HELM, first of several destroyers to clear Pearl Harbor, spots a midget submarine struggling to enter harbor. Shots are fired but miss target. Sub frees itself from reef and submerges.

0825: Using a Browning Automatic Rifle, Lt. Stephen Saltzman and Sgt. Lowell Klatt shoot down an enemy plane making a strafing run on Schofield Barracks.

0826: The Honolulu Fire Department responds to a call for assistance from Hickman Field. 3 firemen are killed and 6 are wounded.

0830: 3rd call is placed for the military via local radio stations.

0835: Tanker NEOSHO, half-loaded with high octane aviation fuel, moves clear of Battleship Row and oil tanks on Ford Island. Damage is reported in the city. Police warn civilians to leave the streets and to return to their homes.

0839: Seaplane tender CURTISS sights midget sub in harbor and commences to fire on it. Destroyer MONAGHAN heads for intruder at ramming speed.

0840: The submarine surfaces after sustaining damage. MONAGHAN hits sub and drops depth charges as she passes. The first explanation is announced over the local radio stations, "A sporadic air attack; rising sun sighted on wing tips."

0850: Lt. Commander Shimazaki orders deployment of 2nd wave of aircraft over military bases on Oahu.

0854: Attack run of planes begins. Fifty-four high-level bombers hit Naval air stations, 78 dive bombers hit ships in Pearl Harbor, 36 fighters circle over harbor to maintain air control.

0900: Crew of the Dutch liner JAGERSFONTEIN opens up with her guns, the first Allies to join the fight. Radios throughout the island crack out urgent messages to the public: "Get off roads and stay off. Don't block traffic. Stay at home. This is the real McCoy."

0930: Tremendous explosions rock the destroyer SHAW, sending debris everywhere. Bomb falls near the Governor's home.

1000: First wave of planes arrives back on carriers, 190 miles north of Oahu.

1005: Governor Poindexter calls local papers, announcing state of emergency for entire territory of Hawaii.

1030: Mayor's Major Disaster Council meets at city hall. Reports from the local hospitals pour in, listing civilian casualties.

1100: Commander Fuchida circles over Pearl Harbor and assesses damage. He then returns to the carrier task force. All schools on Oahu are ordered to close.

1115: A state of emergency is announced over the radio by Governor Poindexter.

1142: As per orders by army, local stations go off the air. General Short confers with the Governor regarding martial law.

1146: The first of many false sightings of enemy troops is made and announced to the public.

1210: American planes fly north in search of enemy troops, with negative results.

1230: Honolulu police raid the Japanese embassy and find the personnel burning documents. A blackout, to begin at nightfall, is ordered by the U.S. Army.

1240: The Governor confers with President Roosevelt regarding martial law. Both agree it is necessary that the military take over the civilian government.

1300: Commander Fuchida lands on board carrier AKAGI. A discussion follows with Admiral Nagumo and staff concerning feasibility of launching 3rd wave of planes.

1330: Signal flags on carrier AKAGI orders the Japanese task force to withdraw. Hawaiian territorial director of civil defense orders blackout every night until further notice.

1458: Tadao Fuchikami delivers message from Washington. The message is decoded and given to General Short. It is an ultimatum from Japan, to be given at 1300 Washington time. General Short orders, "Just what significance the hour set may have we do not know, but be on the alert accordingly."

1625: The Governor signs a Proclamation, and martial law is put into effect.

b) Ramifications: Japanese-Americans
1. U.S. enters World War II
2. U.S. suspicion of Japanese heightened
3. Relocation of some Japanese-Americans

C. World War II
- a) The approach to war
- b) The War Years
  1. September 1939
  2. January 1940
  3. January 1941
  4. January 1942
  5. January 1943
  6. January 1944
  7. January 1945
- c) European Theater of War
- d) Pacific Theater of War
- e) The Aftermath

3. The following table gives a comparison of dates and times for the attacks on Pearl Harbor and Hong Kong. What would have been your local time and date for these two events?

	Local Time	Washington DC Time	London Time
Pearl Harbor	0755, 7 Dec.	1255, 7 Dec.	1755, 7 Dec.
Hong Kong	0800, 8 Dec.	1900, 7 Dec.	2400, 7 Dec.

4. The following people are associated with the bombing of Pearl Harbor. Choose one to study in depth. Share your information with others.

   Hirohito—emperor of Japan at the time of World War II

   Hull, Cordell—Secretary of State of the United States during World War II; was in negotiations with the Japanese when the news of the attack on Pearl Harbor reached him

   Kimmel, Admiral Husband E.—commander of the U.S. Pacific fleet

   Roosevelt, Franklin D.—President of the United States from 1933-1945, he did not live to see the end of the war.

   Short, General Walter C.—military governor of the Hawaiian territory

   Stimson, Henry L.—Secretary of State of the United States before World War II; he urged an international boycott of Japan after it invaded Manchuria.

   Tojo, Hideki—a general and the Premier of Japan during World War II

   Yamamoto, Isoroku—Admiral and commander in chief of Japan's navy; he spoke to some of his friends about the plan of attack on Pearl Harbor in 1941.
5. Interview the senior citizens in your area who have memories of December 7, 1941. If possible, make audio or video records of the interviews so that they may be shared with others. Keep on file.
6. Use the creative medium of your choice to express the thoughts that you have when reading this saying:

   "In war, all suffer defeat, even the victors."
7. Create your own haiku poem. The haiku is a tiny verse form in which Japanese poets have been working for hundreds of years.

   Things to remember about the Japanese haiku:
   a) There are three lines of verse.
   b) The verse contains seventeen syllables.
   c) The first and third lines have five syllables each.
   d) The second line contains seven syllables.
   e) The name of a season, or a key word identifying the season, is often in the haiku.
   f) The haiku is not expected to always be a complete or even a clear statement. The reader adds his/her own associations and imagery, becoming a co–creator.

   The following is a haiku written by the Japanese poet Buson.

   See the morning breeze
   Ruffling his so silky hair...
   Cool caterpillar

8. Write an original poem using the senryu form. This is in the haiku form, but is different in that it is generally not about nature or the seasons of the year. Use a character or event from *Under the Blood-Red Sun* as the topic of your senryu poem.

Line 1	5 syllables
Line 2	7 syllables
Line 3	5 syllables

9. Do some research about your own cultural heritage or one that is of interest to you. Share with the group some information that you have discovered.
10. Tomi thinks that Grampa will tell Papa about the flag incident, "and the story would be much bigger by then." (page 5) Write a sentence or two about a common event. Then turn the event into an elaborate short story. (Read *McElligott's Pool* by Dr. Seuss.)
11. Tomi refers to "bad luck bananas," Lucky, the dog, and Billy, a haole, as bad luck on the boat. (page 42) Make a list of all of the things you can think of that people consider to be bad luck. Research bad luck superstitions. How did some of them come into being? Share your information with the group.
12. Form groups according to interest, to research a major league baseball team. Plan a creative way to present findings to the group, such as a parody of a play, a television news magazine, or a television news interview.
13. Read again pages mid-139 through mid-141. Use prose or poetry to tell about the relationship the author has pictured between Kimi and Tomi.
14. On page 172, the movement of the army trucks is described as "rushed," and the movement of the tanks is described as "thundered." Make a list of as many words as possible that describe movement. Use six of the words in descriptive sentences.
    Example of movement words: fall, flop, hobble, hop, jiggle, jump, prance, race, rock, roll, skip, spin, stride, swing, walk, wiggle…

Vocabulary Word Search Puzzle

Directions: Do the word search. Find the words that may be printed forwards, backwards, horizontally, vertically, and on a diagonal. Write down the letters that have not been used, starting at the top and working left to right in each row. Group the letters into words to find the hidden message.

Some other things to do:

1. Put the words in alphabetical order.
2. Number the words and:
   - Define every odd-numbered word.
   - Use every even-numbered word in a sentence.

P	O	W	S	D	P	I	M	E	S	H	C	R	E	Y	H	S	U	P
T	E	Y	D	C	E	R	N	N	E	R	I	R	E	L	W	A	R	Y
M	I	D	L	E	I	H	O	F	O	L	D	D	I	F	K	S	T	H
A	E	L	E	T	T	T	C	N	R	I	B	E	E	N	O	C	F	R
L	E	F	L	T	P	N	A	N	U	A	T	I	T	L	G	R	I	E
L	S	F	D	E	B	U	I	N	E	N	C	A	D	R	T	E	M	S
E	U	A	O	M	R	E	R	U	A	L	C	T	G	E	E	T	D	T
T	C	G	O	E	E	M	D	B	Q	F	C	I	I	I	R	V	A	A
L	O	Y	M	I	S	K	E	N	A	S	D	N	A	O	R	C	A	R
O	F	S	R	R	I	O	F	U	I	E	O	E	S	T	N	R	N	R
F	S	A	A	E	V	R	D	O	D	I	L	C	D	D	I	S	I	I
T	E	E	W	E	E	E	S	N	T	B	O	I	E	S	E	O	M	W
S	G	U	S	N	V	D	E	A	I	R	S	V	L	U	M	A	N	S
T	R	Q	Z	E	I	H	I	X	N	G	O	O	G	A	S	E	Y	D
A	A	Y	I	M	E	L	E	F	R	T	U	O	C	S	S	M	E	N
C	B	L	A	R	I	L	U	A	I	C	L	H	I	T	B	M	D	E
T	E	R	P	M	F	L	C	O	H	A	E	V	E	O	O	C	I	S
R	Y	P	U	N	L	E	N	E	I	T	E	E	L	O	W	A	K	E
P	A	H	I	Y	D	I	D	D	E	O	M	N	L	S	T	I	R	G

CLENCHED
DEVOTION
ESTEEM
FANATICS
GRIT
HUMILIATION
INFLEXIBLE
IRRIGATION
LOFTS
REFORM
SLOUCHED
SQUINTED
MESH
SYMBOL
SICKLE
WARY
LOOMED
TILLER
WAKE
SWARM
FRENZY
MALLET
GAFF

FOCUS
AVERTED
MACHETE
DIALOGUE
RATTLED
SCORNFULLY
MASSIVE
INCREDIBLE
EERIE
PRONUNCIATION
CRINGED
VISE
ABRUPTLY
APPREHENDED
INFRACTIONS
DISGRACED
PYRAMIDS
PUSHY
TACT
INDEBTED
RELIEVED
BARGES
QUEASY

Vocabulary Crossword Puzzle

Directions: Use the clues to figure out the answers to the crossword puzzle.

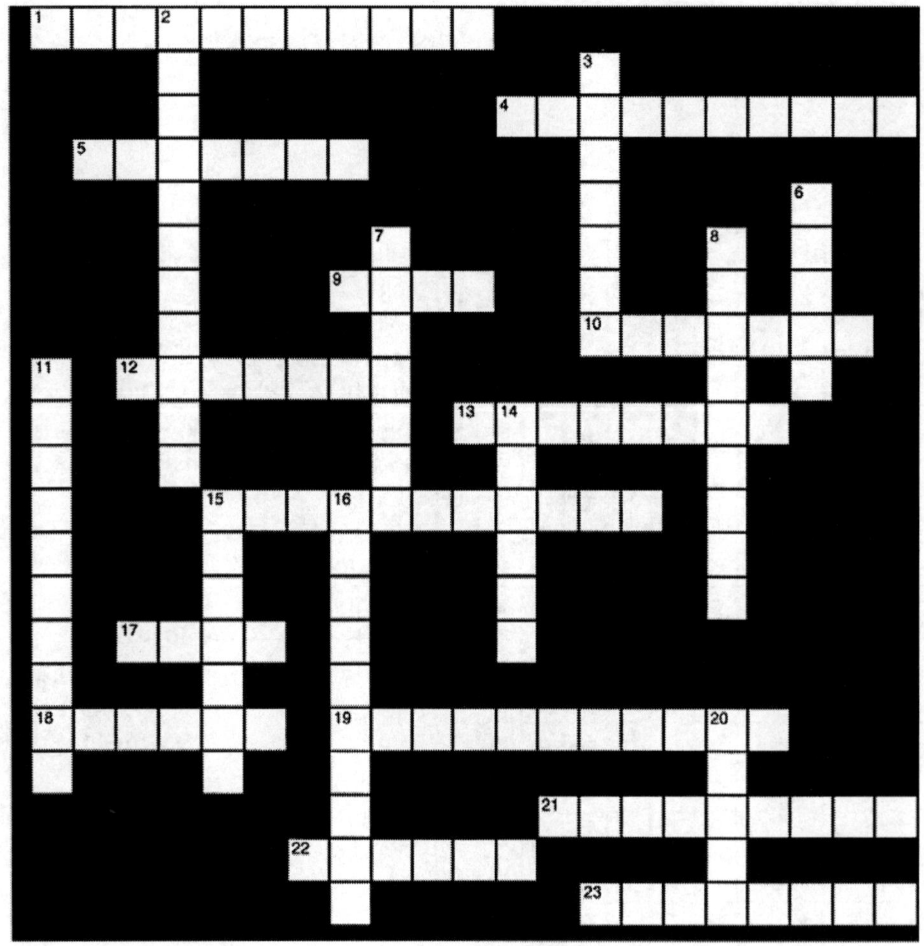

Down

2 violations
3 flinched
6 clarify
7 large
8 shaking
11 beyond belief
14 pounced
15 avoided
16 courteous
20 spooky

Across

1 embarrassment
4 ridged
5 chase
9 finesse
10 obedient
12 groups of vehicles
13 grasped
15 seized
17 cautious
18 appeared
19 disguised
21 dishonored
22 hodgepodge
23 obligated

Bibliography

ABC News. *Pearl Harbor: Two Hours That Changed The World.* (Videorecording) NY: MPI Home Video, 1991. VHS, 85 minutes.
Black, Wallace. *Pearl Harbor.* NY: Crestwood House, 1991.
Dunnahoo, Terry. *Pearl Harbor: America Enters the War.* NY: Franklin Watts, 1991.
Hookinson, Deborah. *Pearl Harbor.* NY: Dillon Press, 1991.
Stein, R. Conrad. *The Story of the U.S.S. Arizona.* Chicago, IL: Children's Press, 1992.
Sullivan, George. *The Day Pearl Harbor Was Bombed: A Photo History of World War II.* NY: Scholastic, 1991.
Target Series. *Pearl Harbor, December 7, 1941.* (Videorecording) Los Angeles, CA: JZ Communications, 1991. VHS, 70 minutes.

Resource Information

The Superintendent
U.S.S. Arizona Memorial
#1 Arizona Memorial Place
Honolulu, Hawaii 96818

Assessment Answers

7. The military of the United States arrest Papa and send him to the camp located on Sand Island. Papa is later sent to the Mainland.
8. Sanji is Papa's friend. He fishes with Papa. Sanji is killed by U.S. gunfire.
9. The katana is the family sword. It is part of the family tradition, representing those of the past, present and future.
10. According to Mr. Ramos, power is the "freedom to make our own choices." (page 235)

Puzzle Answers

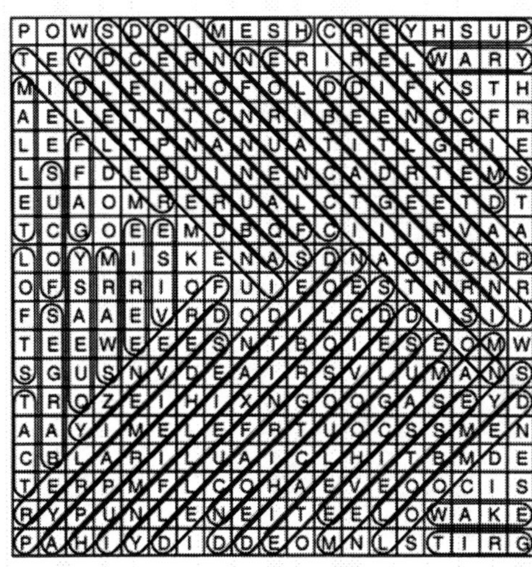

Hidden Message: POWER IS THE FREEDOM TO MAKE OUR OWN DECISIONS

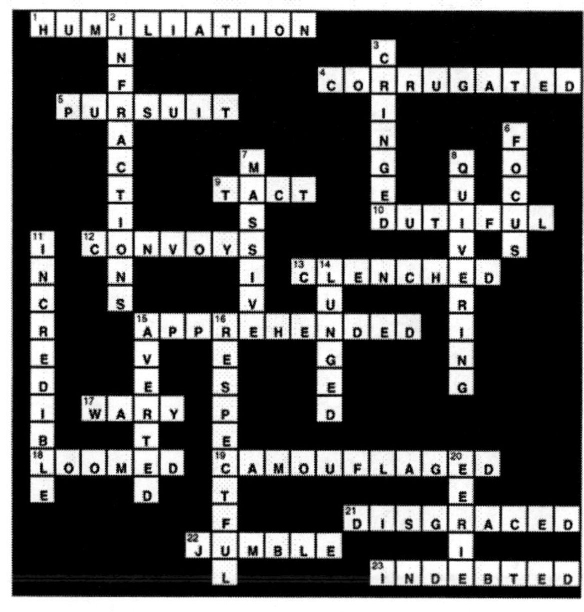

Assessment for *Under the Blood-Red Sun*

Assessment is an on-going process. The following ten items can be completed during the novel study. When an item is completed, the student places the date of completion on the line that is next to it under the STUDENT column. When the teacher and the student check the item together, the date is placed on the line that is next to it under the TEACHER column.

Name ____

Student	Teacher		
______	______	1.	Summarize the story.
______	______	2.	Define the word **friend**.
______	______	3.	Complete two of the vocabulary activities.
______	______	4.	Make an attribute web for your favorite story character.
______	______	5.	What does Papa mean when he tells Tomi, "If you shame yourself, you shame all of us"?
______	______	6.	Explain the significance to the story of Grampa's flag from Japan.
______	______	7.	Who sends Papa to Sand Island? Why?
______	______	8.	Who is Sanji? What happens to him?
______	______	9.	What is the *katana*? Why is it important to the Nakaji family?
______	______	10.	What is Mr. Ramos' definition of **power**?